HOW TO WRITE A NOVEL THAT MATTERS

CRAFTING STORIES WITH THE POWER TO CAPTIVATE, ENLIGHTEN, AND INSPIRE

MIKE KLAASSEN

Copyright © 2024 by Michael John Klaassen

Published independently by Mike Klaassen
www.mikeklaassen.com
Printed in the United States of America

All rights reserved. No part of this publication may be reproduced, distributed, or transmitted in any form or by any means, including photocopying, recording, or other electronic or mechanical methods, without the prior written permission of the publisher, except in the case of brief quotations embodied in critical reviews and certain other noncommercial uses permitted by copyright law.

Paperback edition ISBN: 9781734488784
eBook edition ISBN: 9781734488791

CONTENTS

Acknowledgments   5
Inspiration   9

1. Introduction   13
2. Defining Theme   19
3. Fiction As Art   25
4. Themes Of Plot, Character, Setting, And Style   39
5. Genre   57
6. Message Themes, Part 1—Fiction-Writing Modes   61
7. Message Themes, Part 2—Symbols   67
8. Message Themes, Part 3—Allegory   75
9. Message Vs. Propaganda   85
10. Strategies For Message Development   105
11. Expressing Theme   117
12. Analysis Of A Bestseller   127
13. Theme-Analysis Template   137
14. Theme-Analysis Template—Simple Story   143
15. Theme-Analysis Template—Complex Story   149
16. Troubleshooting A Manuscript For Theme   167
17. Fiction That Matters   187

Also By Mike Klaassen   197
About the Author   199
Bibliography   201
Index   205
Notes   211

ACKNOWLEDGMENTS

I thank my wife, Gerri, for her loving encouragement and support, which made this book possible. I also appreciate the encouragement and support of my friend and fellow author, L. D. Alford.

Dedicated to you: the authors, teachers, and students committed to improving the craft of writing fiction.

INSPIRATION

Early in my writing career, I was fortunate to read *Character Dynamics* by Nancy Kress, whose many words of wisdom include the following.

> "*Theme.* The most fraught word in literature. Even if you rename it *central concern* or *reader resonance* or some such thing, it still conjures memories of ninth-grade English: *What is the book's theme? Concisely state the theme, and be sure to support your statement with specific examples in a well-written essay with topic sentence and—*
>
> "No wonder so many writers go out of their way to announce that their fiction has no theme. They don't want students forced to reduce their works to twenty-five-words-or-less platitudes.

"Nonetheless, every work of fiction does indeed have a theme. … And as a writer, you often benefit from knowing what yours is."[1]

—Nancy Kress, *Character Dynamics*

SPOILER ALERT

This book includes reference to the specifics of bestselling novels, including:

- *Then She Was Gone* by Lisa Jewell
- *A Time for Mercy* by John Grisham
- *Water for Elephants* by Sara Gruen
- *The Underground Railroad: A Novel* by Colson Whitehead
- *The Hotel Nantucket* by Elin Hilderbrand
- *Ready Player One* by Ernest Cline
- *The Da Vinci Code* by Dan Brown
- *The Girl on the Train* by Paula Hawkins
- *The Four Winds* by Kristin Hannah
- *One Italian Summer* by Rebecca Serle
- *The Midnight Library* by Matt Haig
- *The Stranger in the Lifeboat* by Mitch Albom
- *The Last Thing He Told Me* by Laura Dave
- *Wish You Were Here* by Jodi Picoult
- *It Ends With Us* by Colleen Hoover
- *Where the Crawdads Sing* by Delia Owens
- *Lessons in Chemistry* by Bonnie Garmus

1

INTRODUCTION

Some works of fiction fade into obscurity, lost in the sea of forgettable tales, while others leave an indelible mark on our minds, echoing through the corridors of our thoughts for days, months, or even years. In other words, they *resonate*. These stories have the power to stir our emotions, stimulate our intellect, and, in essence, matter profoundly to us. If you aspire to craft novels that possess this enduring quality, join me as we explore the art of storytelling.

Resonance propels a work of fiction toward *transcendence*,[1] in which a work goes beyond our expectations, rising above the competition. Whether or not fiction achieves transcendence varies somewhat from reader to reader, and different works stand out for different reasons, but outstanding works share at least some common factors. I believe those common factors are best explained in the context of theme.

Why should you care? According to John Gardner, "No one can hope to write really well if he has not learned to analyze fiction—how to recognize a symbol when it jumps at him, how to make out theme in a literary work, how to account for a writer's selection and organization of fictional details."[2] Many years ago, I set a personal goal of developing a written model that explains how fiction really works. If you've read my other books about the craft of writing fiction, you already know that I believe five fundamental elements comprise all written fiction: plot, character, setting, style, and theme.[3] For those of us seeking to write the very best we can, understanding plot, character, setting, and style is not enough. We must understand every aspect of fiction, and that includes theme.

Many books about the craft of writing fiction don't even mention the concept of theme or only address it briefly. One of my objectives for this book is to provide the most comprehensive and accurate explanation of theme available anywhere.

Why should you care about theme? A thorough understanding of theme will help you understand why some fiction pleases and some does not, and why one story can stick with you long after you've read it, possibly even changing your life. If you're a writer of fiction, a thorough understanding of theme will help you write more entertaining fiction, possibly even fiction that has the power to influence readers to behave in a manner that improves their life.

Theme is also important to an author's success. A strong theme gives a novel more "weight," more credibility, and readers will recognize this when writing their Amazon reviews. High Amazon ratings inspire future book browsers to buy the book.

Some believe an author may ignore theme because theme develops naturally as a story is told. While there is truth to that, I recall what Evan Marshall wrote in *The Marshall Plan for Novel Writing*: "The way to write successful, salable fiction is to know what you're doing and why at all times; then you won't accidentally do the wrong things in the wrong places."[4] If we're serious about writing fiction in today's competitive publishing environment, we should leave nothing to chance in our effort to create the best stories possible. That means it isn't good enough to write as well as bestselling authors; to compete, we must write even better.

No matter how familiar you are with the concept of theme, or whether you're a writer, teacher, or student of fiction, this book will help you build a foundation of practical knowledge that might otherwise take many years of self-study or trial and error to accumulate.

If you're a student, this book offers understanding unavailable anywhere else. If you're a teacher, this book may provide insight that makes your job easier and more rewarding. If you're a writer, this book may provide you with information that helps you take your writing to new heights or sustains it in the face of ever-increasing competition. You will learn how to plan, write, and revise a manuscript with theme in mind. Lastly, you will learn how to troubleshoot a draft for theme, which can help make it the best that it can be.

Most writers will never be bestselling authors. Novels attain bestseller status for a variety of reasons, some of which are beyond the author's control, but there is one thing over which we, as authors, have absolute control, and that is the quality of our work. The information in this book puts you a giant step closer to bringing your writing to its full potential.

A worthwhile goal for all of us is to write fiction that transcends. This book offers no secret formula or magic solution for writing great fiction, but it does explore theme in new ways, not only studying what theme is, but how it functions, how it can be analyzed, and how it can be developed. The fact that you have opened this book, even if merely to peek inside, tells me that you have a strong interest in how fiction works. My guess is that you are either a writer, a teacher, or a student of the craft of writing fiction. If you're like me, you're all three. Join me now in exploring theme and what makes a work of fiction matter.

TAKEAWAYS

- To matter, stories must have resonance, a quality of fiction shared by works of fiction achieving transcendence.
- *Resonance* is the quality or state of echoing back to the reader emotionally or intellectually, lingering in the mind, causing the reader to mentally revisit the story, reliving it.[5]
- *Transcendent* is the term for fiction that goes beyond or exceeds the usual limits.

The next chapter defines theme and its many forms.

2

DEFINING THEME

Like so many terms used in the craft of writing fiction, *theme* means different things to different people. Definitions and descriptions of *theme* include intangibles such as the meaning or message of the story; or its underlying principle or central concern; or the big idea or driving force. Some authors claim that the theme of a story is its subject matter while others are just as adamant that the subject matter of a story is *not* its theme.

The definition of *theme* in Roget's II thesaurus includes "What a ... piece of writing ... is about," which is as broad a definition as I can imagine. Not all writing is fiction, so for the purposes of this book, I revised this definition to "What a work of written fiction is about." This definition offers writers little help in creating fiction, so why bring it to your attention? Because a broad definition of theme provides us with a place to start. From here, we can deconstruct the concept and examine its components, which will help us achieve the greatest understanding.

What a work of written fiction is about may be viewed from two broad levels: (1) *structural themes*—the *inputs* of plot, character, setting, and style; and (2) *themes of effect*—the *outputs* of the project, the effect on the reader's heart and mind. Of the two, you are probably most familiar with the structural themes, which from my research may be divided into three categories.

- *Micro-themes*: words, punctuation, sentences, and paragraphs
- *Meso-themes*: passages (which include scenes and sequels), acts, and chapters
- *Macro-themes*: plot, character, setting, theme, style, and story

MICRO-THEMES

Do words have themes? Of course. The themes of a word may be found in a dictionary, as definitions. If you doubt that each form of punctuation has its own theme, then you need to read Noah Lukeman's *A Dash of Style: The Art and Mastery of Punctuation*. The themes of a sentence may be found in its subject, verb, object, adjectives, and adverbs. A paragraph's theme can be found in its topic, which may be spelled out in the form of a topic sentence at the beginning or a summary at the end.

Writing is largely about *selectivity*, and choice of micro-themes should—as much as practical or possible—reflect the story's theme. For instance, maybe the theme of a story is "Sometimes being a prick is all a man has left." Then certain word choices and punctuation could reflect that. The character could sigh and huff and swear a lot, or you could end sentences with ellipses.

MESO-THEMES

I define a *passage (or segment) of writing* as two or more consecutive paragraphs with a common purpose.[1] Passages of writing may be classified into four types: (1) scenes, (2) sequels, (3) passages that include elements of both scenes and sequels, and (4) passages that are neither scenes nor sequels.[2]

I define an *act* as a sequence of closely related written passages,[3] and I define a *chapter* as a passage or segment of writing delineated by chapter breaks.[4] Passages, acts, and chapters are *structural units of fiction* and may include just about anything as content. The common denominator of that content would also be that structural unit's theme.

To the extent practical or possible, the choice of meso-themes should reflect the themes of a story. For example, Lee Child's Jack Reacher series includes scenes and sequels that support themes such as the powerful have an obligation to help the less fortunate, justice prevails, and sometimes the end justifies the means.

MACRO-THEMES

The five fundamental elements that comprise all written fiction are plot, character, setting, style, and theme.[5] Each of the fundamental elements has its own specific function:

1. *Plot* is what happens.
2. *Character* is the who.
3. *Setting* is the where and when.
4. *Style* is the how.
5. *Theme* is the why.[6]

Even though each of the fundamental elements has its own function, each may also influence and contribute to the others. For example, characters influence plot, plot shapes character, setting may act as a character or obstruct a character's attempt to achieve a goal, a myriad of stylistic choices made by the author mold each of the other elements, and each of the other elements contributes to themes.

Together, the five elements comprise a story. The messages of a story are not only part of theme; they may also influence plot, character, setting, and style.

TAKEAWAYS

- *Theme* is what a work of written fiction is about.
- *Theme* is the *why* of fiction.
- Themes may be viewed in two broad categories: (1) themes of structure, and (2) themes of effect.

- Structural themes may be classified as (1) micro-themes—for words, punctuation, sentences, and paragraphs; (2) meso-themes—for passages, acts, and chapters; and (3) macro-themes—for plot, character, setting, theme, style, and story.
- Even though each of the fundamental elements has its own function, each may also influence and contribute to the others.
- Together, the five fundamental elements comprise a story.

Much of this book addresses the macro-structural themes of fiction, but the next chapter focuses on themes of effect—how fiction affects readers: fiction as art.

3

FICTION AS ART

The process of creating fiction is often referred to as a craft, but writing is also an art.[1] To fully understand theme, we must first understand fiction as art. In the middle of the nineteenth century, Edgar Allan Poe referred to writers as artists and fiction as works of literary art. He noted that to render his work universally appreciable, the author needs to create a work of fiction that excites the heart and satisfies the intellect.[2]

A hundred years later, American novelist John Gardner built upon Poe's observations, stating that "An important work of art is at least some of the following: (1) aesthetically interesting, (2) technically accomplished, and (3) intellectually massive."[3]

From these earlier observations, I conclude that one approach to analyzing fiction, including theme, is from these three aspects of art: (1) emotional, (2) intellectual, and (3) technological. Stated differently, fiction as art may be viewed from the perspectives of the heart, the mind, and the craft.

This chapter addresses the emotional and intellectual aspects of fiction as art. The technological considerations, the "how to" of the craft, will be covered later in the book.

WHY WRITE FICTION?

Something every author should ask himself or herself from time to time is: Why do I write? Reasons for writing may be classified as either internal (for the writer's own benefit) or external (for the benefit of others).

First, let's consider the *internal* reasons for writing fiction. Some of us are introverted, inhibited, shy, or socially awkward, making it difficult to communicate verbally. Writing provides an opportunity to express oneself in a way that allows people to feel like a well-functioning social being.

According to Hungarian playwright Lajos Egri, "Without exception, everyone was born with creative ability. It is essential that people be given the opportunity to express themselves … Every human being needs an outlet for his inborn creative talent. If you feel you would like to write, then write."[4]

Another reason to write is that completing a work of fiction, regardless of its quality, may produce a sense of accomplishment or, even better, pride in something done well. Or as Egri notes, "The urge to be outstanding is a fundamental necessity in our lives."[5]

But let's face it: writers are human and, as such, crave attention. As Egri puts it, "We want to be noticed. We want to be remembered. We want to be important! We can achieve a degree of importance by expressing ourselves in the medium which best suits our particular talents."[6]

Another consideration is that writing fiction has the potential, however improbable, for an author to earn a fortune. And for an even longer-term payoff, there is the possibility of creating a work that may be valued by readers long after the author is dead, something of us that can live in perpetuity, a form of immortality.

The *external* reasons for writing fiction are to help readers have a better life and to touch people in a way the author couldn't otherwise. Writing fiction may even be viewed as a form of community service, as in helping the world be a better place.

WHY WE READ FICTION

Just as important as knowing why writers write is to know why readers read. I suspect that most people who habitually read fiction do so simply because they enjoy it. They read one novel after another, written by a handful of authors they like, in genres they enjoy. There's nothing wrong with that: the number one role of fiction is to "transfer an emotional experience to the reader."[7] My favorite authors write historical fiction, thrillers, and sci-fi, and I read these novels for entertainment and relaxation.

Closely related to the role of fiction as a form of entertainment is fiction as a means of relaxation, an escape, a means of stepping away for a few minutes or hours from the reality of daily life, whether it be full of stress, excitement, drudge, or something else. The world of fiction provides an opportunity for our brain to take a break from whatever it deals with routinely and to reorganize itself. A successful reading session may be viewed as a mini vacation, a mental-health break, or a pause that refreshes—like rebooting a computer.

Readers generally select a particular work of fiction for one of two reasons: obligation or choice. Reading may occur out of a sense of obligation, as when someone in authority over readers (such as an employer) influences them to read it. Most likely, all of us have read fiction out of obligation. Students are routinely obligated to assigned reading. The vast majority of adults who read fiction do so by choice, purely of their own free will, with the hope that the experience will be satisfying in some way.

EFFECT OF FICTION

Fiction may have numerous effects on readers: emotion, affirmation, education, instruction, elucidation, inspiration, and motivation.

Emotion And Information

As writers, we stimulate emotion by skillfully selecting and arranging words. In his book *On Moral Fiction*, university professor John Gardner states: "Words conjure emotionally charged images in the reader's mind, and when the words are put together in the proper way, ...we have the queer experience of falling through the print on the page into something like a dream, an imaginary world so real and convincing."[8]

I define *emotive* as the quality of fiction that stimulates the reader's heart. Emotiveness ranges from emotionless to melodramatic. Written fiction may be crafted to generate any emotion, from love to hate, comfort to terror, admiration to disgust. The degree to which a work of fiction is emotive reflects if and how it touches the reader's heart. An example is Kristin Hannah's *The Four Winds*, in which the author portrays Elsa writing in her journal, "Love is what remains when everything else is gone."[9]

I assume that any work of fiction that attracts and retains readers successfully generates an emotional experience valued by its readers. Why else would those readers stick with it to the end and then seek more? Works of fiction that succeed in entertaining readers are worthy of admiration. They are accomplishing their primary objective and providing a vital service to mankind.

The works of fiction I enjoy the most are those that alter my mood, novels that take me out of an everyday, humdrum mindset and transport me to a different feeling; like a train trip through Europe would, or a barefoot stroll along a sandy beach might, or a glass of my favorite wine does. After a good read, I feel different and better.

The emotionally charged, dream-like state described by John Gardner[10] creates an environment within which the reader relaxes his intellectual defenses. In effect, the reader "lowers his guard" and may be receptive to new ideas and information. I believe that any work of fiction that successfully entertains its reader also stimulates an intellectual response.

To understand how this works, we need to compare fiction to the real world. The imaginary world of fiction is quite different than real life, which flows past us in a blur, with much happening at once.[11] Art is all about the selection and condensation of concepts into capsule form that may be more easily digested by the reader.[12] Fiction can take a fragment of reality and examine it from a different angle, providing a new perspective.

For example, like me, you probably have a perception of how a hotel operates but haven't given much thought to the particulars. In *The Hotel Nantucket*, Elin Hilderbrand gives the reader a behind-the-scenes look, from administration to housekeeping to the front desk. From the perspective of numerous employees, Hilderbrand spins a web of subplots that weave the lives of personnel into business operations. This novel enriched my appreciation for how the hospitality industry delivers its service, changing my perspective on the subject.

Viewed through the lens of fiction, any concept may be studied. Fiction creates order, compared to the chaos of real life. Fiction may also be viewed as a mental simulation within which we can immerse ourselves, experiencing imaginary events as if we are living them ourselves. All the above flow through the reader's mind as information.

Whether or not the reader consciously realizes that she is receiving information, her mind takes it in and processes it. The mind can't help but do this because that's one of its primary functions. Inevitably, this information generates an intellectual response as the mind either accepts it, rejects it, or modifies it.

Popular fiction is sometimes criticized as being all about entertainment and, therefore, lacking intellectual involvement. Nothing could be further from the truth. Whether you call it popular fiction or commercial fiction or genre fiction, these works, read by millions around the world, have a huge intellectual influence on their readers in the form of affirmation.

Affirmation

Affirmation[13] validates, confirms, or reinforces what we already know or believe. John Gardner wrote: "It is precisely because art affirms values that it is important."[14] Gloria Kempton says, "If you validate your reader, he'll love you and read anything you write for the rest of his life. Yes, one of the reasons a reader chooses to read a story in the first place is because he needs validation. This is often at an unconscious level."[15]

Literary agent Donald Maass wrote: "Most readers are moral people. They turn to fiction—really, to any form of storytelling—for affirmation of the values we hold in common. They long to know what they believe is right. Contemporary life offers few opportunities to take a strong moral stand, but fiction deals heavily with such moments."[16]

I believe that most stories are *affirmative*, supporting a pre-existing belief of its likely readers. Most of us prefer stories that are consistent with our strongest beliefs, rather than those that tell us we are wrong. Think about some of the values commonly affirmed in fiction:

- Love conquers all.
- Persistence leads to success.
- Justice prevails.

These values are routinely demonstrated in novels of all types, including fantasy, romance, westerns, thrillers, horror, and crime. Fiction illustrates the worthiness or legitimacy of the reader's concerns by demonstrating those values in the form of a story.

Over time, values and opinions change. For example, even a casual survey of national news today highlights frightening concerns about:

- Mistreating the environment
- Artificial intelligence
- Emergence of a totalitarian government

The opposite of affirmative is *refutative*, which tends to overthrow a concept by argument, evidence, or proof.[17] Themes in fiction may challenge the reader's preconception, causing him to re-examine his stand or position or the accuracy of his information. Some of the most successful novels are refutative. In

The Da Vinci Code, Dan Brown turns classic perceptions of Mary Magdalene and the Holy Grail on their head. In *A Time for Mercy*, John Grisham builds a theme refuting the concept that premeditated murder should always be punished. A theme in *Where the Crawdads Sing* by Delia Owens is that cold-blooded murder may not be immoral, just part of nature. Mitch Albom, in *The Stranger in the Lifeboat*, portrays God differently than I suspect many believe.

Fiction can also produce intellectual involvement through education, instruction, elucidation, inspiration, and motivation.

Education

People love to learn, and fiction provides an enjoyable context for *education*,[18] learning new facts. I love reading historical fiction portraying events of the past in a manner that educates me about another time and place, especially a crossroads in history. Dan Brown's *The Da Vinci Code* is filled with symbology, art history, and religion. *Where the Crawdads Sing* by Delia Owens is steeped in information about a Carolina coastal swamp. Sara Gruen's *Water for Elephants* portrays the everyday operations of a circus during the Great Depression. Reading informative, or *educational*, fiction is a fun way to learn stuff.

Instruction

In addition to learning facts, new skills may be acquired through *instruction*.[19] According to John Gardner, "Art instructs. Why, one may wonder, would anyone wish to deny a thing so obvious?"[20] Traditional teaching methods in the medical field include "See one. Do one. Teach one." Reading fiction doesn't offer an opportunity to do one or teach one, but stories abound in examples of readers seeing something done for the first time. Novels I've written portray the main character field-dressing a deer, using a twig as a makeshift compass, and loading a musket. *Instructive* fiction can portray characters doing anything the author chooses: from brain surgery to prosecuting a murderer. Such portrayal may offer the reader only an initial exposure to an activity, but I suspect "seeing" something done in a novel has stimulated countless sparks of interest that eventually grew into hobbies or even careers. For most of us, learning how things work is not just interesting, it can broaden our perspective, helping us become more rounded individuals.

Elucidation

New information may shed light on an issue, in the form of *elucidation*, making sense of life and the world around us. On this subject John Gardner noted, "Art's incomparable ability to ... make alternatives intellectually and emotionally clear, to spotlight falsehood, insincerity, foolishness—art's incomparable ability, that is to make us understand."[21] For those of us who have never lived in a Native-American community, *Firekeeper's Daughter* by Angeline Boulley provides insight into an intriguing world, but it also illuminates issues of humanity, some admirable, others deplorable. I grew up on a farm in

Kansas, but *The Four Winds* by Kristin Hannah is *elucidative*; it opened my eyes to what rural life would have been like during the Dust Bowl of the 1930s.

Inspiration

Fiction can generate *inspiration*,[22] lifting and broadening the human spirit.[23] If a work of fiction pumps up a person—positive inspiration—for a few days, it has been very successful. If you watch *It's a Wonderful Life* in the afternoon, you'll feel inspired the rest of the day and maybe into the next morning. Even though life dealt many setbacks to Kya in *Where the Crawdads Sing*, I found the story inspirational in how she dealt with one issue after another.

Motivation

Fiction can also produce *motivation*, inciting readers to action. Regarding motivational fiction, John Gardner wrote, "No one seriously doubts, surely, that Tolstoy's essential argument is right: ideals expressed in art can affect behavior in the world, at least in some people some of the time."[24] According to Noah Lukeman in *The Plot Thickens*,[25] only a select number of works achieve this pinnacle of impact. The most profound effect you can have on your audience is to engage them so deeply with your creation that merely completing it isn't sufficient; you ignite within them a compelling urge to act upon what they've experienced. You might empower them to pursue something they previously lacked the bravery for or reveal to them an injustice they were oblivious to, sparking their outrage. This spectrum of actions they might take can range from deciding to make a change to writing to their political representatives, or even initiating a protest. This represents the supreme influence you possess as a writer. Your power extends beyond merely altering someone's perspective or persuading them of something they once deemed impossible; you may prompt them into tangible action.[26]

According to Gloria Kempton, "If we can learn to consider our readers with every story we write, we can serve them with our fiction in a way that can empower them and change their lives,"[27] and "We want to empower readers to live their best lives, ... lives they can be proud of."[28]

To paraphrase Edgar Allan Poe, the effect of fiction upon readers is a function of how well the writer crafted the work to excite the heart and satisfy the intellect.[29]

TAKEAWAYS

- The process of creating fiction is an art, as well as a craft.
- Fiction may be viewed from three aspects: (1) emotional, (2) intellectual, and (3) technological, i.e., from the perspective of the heart, the mind, and the craft.
- Writers write for internal reasons (to help themselves) and for external reasons (to help others).
- Some readers read out of obligation, but most read because they find it satisfying.

- Fiction may have numerous *effects on readers*: emotion, affirmation, education, instruction, elucidation, inspiration, and motivation.

This chapter addressed the effect that written fiction has on readers. The next two chapters address the structural themes of fiction, starting with plot, character, setting, and style.

4

THEMES OF PLOT, CHARACTER, SETTING, AND STYLE

This chapter addresses four of the five elemental themes of fiction.

THEMES OF PLOT

Plot is what happens in fiction.[1] From making love to making war, events define a work of fiction. Events by themselves, however, do not necessarily rise to the level of a plot. Even a series of events arranged in chronological order may merely comprise a *chronicle*. Only when events are portrayed in a particular manner do they become a plot.

DEFINITION OF PLOT

I define a *plot* as a series of events selected, arranged, and presented in a manner that dramatizes attempts to achieve a goal. The phrase *events selected, arranged, and presented* suggests that not just any old events will do. The definition requires a goal, and that means a character with an objective. Including the word *dramatizes* in the definition implies that the style of the writing is intended to create reader interest, to entertain, and to generate an emotional reaction.

And *the achievement of a goal* (or the failure to do so) generates at least one theme. For example, a woman wants to climb Mount Everest. Whether or not the goal is stated explicitly, the attempt to accomplish something implies a goal. Attempts to achieve the goal will be either successful or not. If successful, a theme of the story is that persistence pays. If unsuccessful, a theme of the story is that even if you persist, you may fail.

PROTOTYPE PLOT

In my book *Third-Person Possessed*, I describe a prototype plot.[2] The beginning of a prototype plot includes a *setup*, or *orientation*,[3] which depicts the character's current situation, largely portraying his world as being in a state of equilibrium—his status quo. The beginning also includes a significant event, or *inciting incident*,[4] [5] that disturbs the character's stability, maybe even turning his world upside down.

After the inciting incident, the character reels with emotion, which reflects his state of mind after his world has been disrupted. When the character's emotions settle down, he enters a phase of *thinking* about what happened, in which he reviews the inciting incident, *analyzes* the new realities of his situation, and considers possible courses of action to take in order to make his world right again. His options are limited because a physical, mental, social, or moral barrier, or *crucible*, prevents him from ignoring the new problem and just walking away from it. The character experiences a *dilemma* in which he contemplates the situation, weighing the probable cost against the potential reward (i.e., the *stakes*) of addressing the problem. The character answers this *call to action*, concluding that he must respond, regardless of the potential risk, and he selects a course of action. The character's decision to take a specific course marks the end of the plot's beginning.

The middle of the prototype plot includes an escalation of drama, sometimes called *rising action*,[6] as the main character encounters increasingly more difficult obstacles that thwart his attempts to achieve his goals. Late in the middle of the story, the character faces his most challenging obstacle so far, and his attempt fails decisively. This failure marks the end of the plot's middle.

The plot's ending begins with the character experiencing devastation in an emotional *dark moment*[7] of despair, also known as the *crisis*.[8] The character feels intimidated when the forces aligned against him seem too powerful to overcome. As the character thinks about his situation, he makes a discovery, possibly through an epiphany, that helps him see his situation in a new light. *Visualization* helps the character plan one last path to success, and then he decides to make this desperate attempt, against all odds, risking everything that's at stake.

The character commences an all-out effort, known as the *climax*,[9] against a seemingly unbeatable force. This battle ends in victory, defeat, or some combination of the two, producing the story's *resolution*. A final passage ties up all loose ends, forming the conclusion, or *denouement*.[10]

PLOT COMPONENTS

Each component of a prototype plot bears the seed of one or more themes. For example, in the beginning of Sara Gruen's *Water for Elephants*, the main character loses his parents, his home, and his intended career, suggesting personal loss as themes. In the middle of the story, the character seems to have found what may be at least a temporary home, a job, and a family, only to be thwarted by a cruel boss, forbidden love, and precarious living conditions, each suggesting potential themes. By the end of the book, the character faces an impossible situation, where he (1) is in love with his boss's wife, whom the main character has impregnated, (2) has been fired from his job, and (3) faces being homeless again, each of which may suggest themes. A story that focuses on a particular plot or portion of a plot could be said to have a theme expressed in terms of that plot or component of plot.

MASTER PLOT

Most plots fit into recognizable patterns, sometimes called *master plots*, as detailed by Ronald B. Tobias in *20 Master Plots (And How to Build Them)*. Some of the plots Tobias lists are external plots and some are internal. I define an *external plot*[11] as a series of events in which a character must overcome an external obstacle (such as another character, a group of characters, society as a whole, or the story's setting) in his attempts to achieve a goal. I define an *internal plot*[12] as a series of events in which a character must overcome an internal obstacle or question, such as a weakness or flaw within himself, to achieve his goal.

Although Tobias doesn't describe master plots in terms of a story goal, each of the master plots features a main character with a primary goal, which may be considered a theme of that plot. For example, in the external master plot of the quest, the character's goal is to find a person, place, or thing, which means that a theme of this master plot is a quest. In the internal master plot of maturation, the goal of the character is to overcome youthful inadequacies, which means maturation is a theme of this type of plot. An example of a novel with a master-plot theme is Lisa Jewell's *Then She Was Gone*, in which the protagonist struggles to learn what happened to her daughter, which means that the master plot theme of this novel is that of a riddle or mystery.

EVENTS

Events may be intellectual, verbal, or physical. Intellectual events occur in the mind and may be in the present (happening in the real-time of the story), in the past (as the character recalls them), or in the future (as the character imagines them). Events (regardless of whether they are verbal, physical, intellectual, present, past, or future) may create themes for a work of fiction.

In my three novels, events provide a catalyst, defining the remainder of the story.

- In *The Brute*, a tornado destroys a campsite, suggesting that disaster is a theme of the story.
- In *Cracks*, an earthquake kills all the adults, suggesting that disaster is a theme of the story.
- In *Backlash*, the United States of America declares war on Great Britain, suggesting that war is a theme of the story.

TAKEAWAYS

- Plot is *what happens* in fiction,[13] but a list of events, even if portrayed in chronological order, may not amount to a plot.
- *Plot* may be defined as a series of events selected, arranged, and presented in a manner that dramatizes attempts to achieve a goal.
- Each component of a prototype plot bears the seed of one or more themes.
- *External plot*[14] may be defined as a series of events in which a character must overcome external obstacles.
- *Internal plot*[15] may be defined as a series of events in which a character must overcome an internal obstacle or question, such as a weakness or flaw within himself, to achieve his goal.
- Many plots fit into recognizable patterns called *master plots*, each of which may be classified by the main character's primary goal, another theme.

THEMES OF CHARACTER

Character is the *who* of fiction.[16] According to John O'Hara, "There is no greater theme than men and women."[17] Ronald B. Tobias, in *Theme & Strategy*, says, "Literature is full of books about people. When a work concentrates on a person (or persons) so that he or she (or they) becomes the center of the plot and action, then the theme of the work is character. *David Copperfield, Madame Bovary, Anne Karenina*, and *The Great Santini* are a few examples of many. Just look in your library for books with people's names in the titles."[18] A more recent example is Taylor Jenkins Reid's *The Seven Husbands of Evelyn Hugo*, in which the main character is a major theme of the novel.

CHARACTERISTICS

Characterization is the act, process, or result of describing the essential quality or nature of a person or personality.[19] A *characteristic* is a trait, quality, or property, or a group of them, distinguishing an individual, group, or type.[20]

As in real life, characters in fiction can be complex individuals. They may be differentiated by physical or intellectual characteristics, any of which may be perceived as neutral, positive, or negative—as strengths or weaknesses.

Any character trait that receives emphasis in a work of fiction may also become a theme. For example, in the Harry Potter series, Harry's lightning-shaped scar and special abilities contribute to the theme of magic. In *The Girl on the Train*,

Rachel's addiction contributes to the story's theme of alcoholism. In *Ready Player One*, Wade's skills contribute to the story's computer-game theme.

In the context of writing fiction, the most important characteristics of a character are those that determine that character's goal. From values spring goals. Without values, the focal character won't accept the challenge created by the inciting incident. If the main character doesn't have a goal, there is no story. Examples of goals that may become themes include vengeance, escape, pursuit, solving a problem, and preventing disaster.

ARCHETYPE CHARACTER

Each of us is a unique person, unlike any before or after us. But also, as in real life, even the most unique among us have similarities to others, certainly to some who came before or after us. An *archetype* is the original model, form, or pattern from which something is made or from which something develops.[21] An *archetype character* is one from which many other characters may be developed.[22] Victoria Lynn Schmidt, in *45 Master Characters: Mythic Models for Creating Original Characters*, says, "To a writer, archetypes are the blueprints for building well-defined characters, be they heroes, villains or supporting characters."[23]

Schmidt's profiles include eight female heroes and their villain counterparts as well as eight male heroes and their villain counterparts. These range from Aphrodite: The Seductive Muse and the Femme Fatale, to Zeus: The King and the Dictator. When a work of fiction focuses on a character that is based on an archetype, then that archetype also becomes a theme.

CHARACTER ARC

Changes that occur in a character (1) at the beginning of the story, (2) during the story, and (3) at the end of the story form that character's arc. A character's arc may become a theme for a character, a story, or a genre. For example, a coming-of-age story is about character change.

TAKEAWAYS

- Character is the *who* of fiction.[24]
- *Characterization* is the act, process, or result of describing the essential quality or nature of a person or personality.[25]
- *Characteristic* is a trait, quality, or property, or a group of them, distinguishing an individual, group, or type.[26]
- *Archetype* is the original model, form, or pattern from which something is made or from which something develops.[27]
- *Archetype character* is one from which many other characters may be developed.[28]
- Any character trait that receives emphasis in a work of fiction may also become a theme.
- *Character arc* refers to the change a character makes during a story.

THEMES OF SETTING

Setting is the *where and when* of a story.[29] Fiction doesn't happen in a vacuum: it has a setting, which at a minimum may be broadly categorized by either place (anywhere in the universe, either real or imaginary) or time (past, present, or future). A story that focuses on a particular setting, whether in time or place or both, could be said to have a theme expressed in terms of that setting. James Mitchener built a career writing novels with setting as the defining theme; examples include *Hawaii, Chesapeake, Poland, Space,* and many more.

Setting includes more than the physical stage of a work of fiction. It also encompasses *milieu*, which means the broader environment in which the fiction is set, including *zeitgeist*: the spirit of the time, or the general intellectual and moral or trend of culture and taste characteristic of an era.[30] For example, Rebecca Serle's *One Italian Summer* is set in Positano, Italy, a location prime for both romance and magic.

A story may be told all in one place, and that place may be in the mind of the character, as in when a character dreams about a place, recalls it, or merely thinks about it.

Setting also includes time. A story must move in time, generally forward in a linear pattern as the story progresses, but if the work of fiction includes time travel, the character moves back and forth in time as the story progresses. And if the author so chooses for dramatic effect, the story may be presented in segments in some order other than chronological, as in the parallel plots of *Where the Crawdads Sing*, where a murder mystery beginning in 1969 is told parallel to Kya's coming-of-age plot, which starts in 1952.

Setting may provide an obstacle to the achievement of the character's goal, suggesting another set of themes:

- A physical barrier, or wildlife, or the weather, as in *man-versus-nature* stories;
- A social barrier, as in *man-versus-society* stories;
- A race against time, the *ticking clock*, which provides an obstacle to achieving a goal before time runs out; and
- Constraining factors, in the form of a physical, a temporal, or a social barrier (or *crucible*), that prevents the character from simply walking away from the inciting incident of the story or individual scenes and sequels.

Setting may also be presented in a manner that makes it resemble a character, as in survival stories where nature takes on the role of an antagonist, thwarting a character's attempt to achieve a goal. In *The Four Winds* by Kristin Hannah, the Depression-era Dust Bowl sucks the life out of farming in the plains states. Or setting may be presented as an ally of the character, such as in *Where the Crawdads Sing*, where the coastal marsh comforts, protects, and instructs Kya as she struggles to survive, or where the roles are reversed when Kya becomes the protector of the swamp, much as a child matures and provides care to a parent. Each of the above aspects of setting may also provide fertile ground for one or more themes of a work of fiction.

Examples of setting in recent bestsellers:

- *A Time for Mercy* by John Grisham: a small town in northern Mississippi
- *The Girl on the Train* by Paula Hawkins: a suburb of London
- *Ready Player One* by Ernest Cline: a futuristic America obsessed with a computer game
- *Water for Elephants* by Sara Gruen: an American circus company during the Great Depression
- *His Dark Materials* by Philip Pullman: a fantastical England, where people have a personal animal spirit and polar bears wear armor
- *The Handmaid's Tale* by Margaret Atwood: a futuristic society in which many wives are not fertile, so young women with reproductive potential are indentured to powerful couples as handmaids

Setting can contribute to the entertainment effect of fiction by functioning as a transporter, whisking the reader from place to place, providing an interesting and exciting background for the story. And fiction can function as a time machine, contributing to the intellectual aspect of reading fiction, providing opportunities for the reader to learn new facts about a particular time place or perspective about a specific era in history. Examples of novels including nonlinear presentation of time include *Wish You Were Here, One Italian Summer,* and *The Midnight Library.*

Any aspect of setting that is emphasized in a story may be viewed as a theme of that work of fiction.

TAKEAWAYS

- Setting is the *where and when* of a story.[31]
- A story that focuses on a particular setting, whether in time or place or both, could be said to have a theme expressed in terms of that setting.
- Setting encompasses *milieu*, which means the broader environment in which the fiction is set, including *zeitgeist* (the spirit of the time), or the general intellectual, moral, and cultural climate of an era.[32]
- Setting includes time, which must generally move forward in a linear pattern as the story progresses, but if the work of fiction includes time travel, the character moves back and forth in time as the story progresses.
- If the author so chooses for dramatic effect, the story may be presented in segments in some order other than chronological.
- Setting may provide an obstacle to the achievement of the character's goal.
- Setting may be presented in a manner that makes it resemble a character.
- Any aspect of setting that is emphasized in a story may be viewed as a theme of that work of fiction.

THEMES OF STYLE

In the words of John Gardner, "The last major element that may modify thought is *style*."[33] Style is the *how* of a story.[34] A story presented with a particular emphasis or innovation in style has a theme defined by that style. When referring to works in which "the author's style becomes the focus of the work," Ronald B. Tobias, in *Theme & Strategy*, says, "The work may still include all the basic elements of good storytelling, but plot, character, and action take a back seat to this expression of style."[35]

The fundamental element of style is the composite effect of a myriad of choices made by an author during the process of creating a story.[36] Those choices involve fiction-writing modes, scenes and sequels, story structure, narrative package, and many more. When and if any of these choices are emphasized to the point they bring attention to themselves, they become a theme of the work of fiction. Here's an example from William Faulkner's *As I Lay Dying*.

> The quilt is drawn up to her chin, hot as it is, with only her two hands and her face outside. She is propped on the pillow, with her head raised so she can see out the window, and we can hear him every time he takes up the adze of the saw. If we were deaf we could almost watch her face and hear him, see him. Her face is wasted away so that the bones draw just under the skin in white lines. Her eyes are like two candles when you watch them gutter down to sockets of iron candle-sticks. But the eternal and the everlasting salvation and grace is not upon her.[37]

Most of the novels I studied for this book presented plot, character, and setting in an unobtrusive manner. Style in fiction may range from unobtrusive (in which a casual reader may ask,

"What style?") to so obtrusive that it may rival the other fundamental elements—even to the point of overwhelming the reader's attention, in either a positive way or negative.

At least three of the novels I analyzed for this book were crafted in such an unobtrusive style that only by looking closely could I detect stylish distraction: *A Time for Mercy*, *Ready Player One*, and *Water for Elephants*.

Many novels fall midway along the obtrusiveness range, largely dominated by relatively unobtrusive presentation yet featuring an aspect of style that stands out. For example, much of *The Girl on the Train* by Paula Hawkins is presented unobtrusively, but one aspect of style jumped out at me: this novel is written in first-person narration—from the point of view of *three* female characters. Another example is *Where the Crawdads Sing*, in which the chronological timeline of the story is chopped in two and presented in alternating chapters as parallel subplots. One book, Colson Whitehead's Pulitzer Prize-winning *The Underground Railroad*, stands out by including characters and passages that have little, if anything, to do with the rest of the story, a style that is so obtrusive that it distracted me from the admirable aspects of the novel.

Another quality of style in fiction is its potential *effectiveness* in helping the reader *suspend disbelief* to the degree that she can feel as if she is experiencing the story as if it were real. I had little trouble suspending disbelief as I read *A Time for Mercy*, *Ready Player One*, and *Water for Elephants*.

In *The Girl on the Train*, first-person narration for the main character, Rachel, was a reasonable choice, but also narrating in first-person from the perspective of two other female characters was, I felt, confusing and annoying—and totally unnecessary. Multiple first-person narration is a stylistic innovation that, in my opinion, detracts from the positive resonance of the rest of the story.

By contrast, in *Where the Crawdads Sing*, the decision to split the storyline and tell the murder mystery as a parallel plot was a beneficial stylistic choice for dramatic effect. Without the parallel plot presentation, in which the body of Chase Andrews is discovered in the prologue, I may have lost interest in the story long before the murder, which doesn't happen until halfway through the story's chronological timeline. In this case, a stylistic choice contributed to the positive resonance of the novel.

Returning to the concept that written fiction is art, consider musical composition. Sounds, or musical notes, comprise a song. Using a variety of instruments and vocals or both, composers have arranged and rearranged the same notes for centuries—nothing new there. The originality of a piece of music derives from the creativity and skill with which the composer organizes the notes in a manner that delights and moves the audience.

As with musical notes, there really aren't any new styles in written fiction. Innovation and profoundness come from the creativity and skill of the author in arranging the words. For example, consider the story themes in *Where the Crawdads Sing*: survival, coming of age, romance, ascension, and murder mystery, each of which have been used countless times as master plots since the emergence of written fiction. Whether or not a story resonates with the reader depends upon the combination of creativity and skill that comes together in the many choices made by the author—his or her style in presenting the tale.

TAKEAWAYS

- Style is the *how* of fiction.[38]
- A story presented with a particular emphasis or innovation in style has a theme defined by that style.
- The fundamental element of style is the composite effect of myriad choices made by an author during the process of creating a story.[39]
- Style may range in *obtrusiveness* from unobtrusive (What style?) to very obtrusive (distracting).
- Style may range in *effectiveness* from being very effective in helping suspend disbelief to very ineffective.
- Stylistic innovation may contribute to the positive resonance of a work or detract from it.

The next chapter addresses genre as it relates to theme.

5

GENRE

In the words of John Gardner, "The artist's primary unit of thought—his primary conscious or unconscious basis for selecting and organizing the details of his work—is genre."[1] The word *genre* means category,[2] and the universe of written fiction includes many broad categories, ranging from romance to horror, historical to sci-fi, juvenile to adult, and humorous to literary. I define *genre* as works of fiction that have one or more themes in common.

Genre may be best understood within the context of fundamental themes, with each genre being defined by its dominant fundamental element. More specifically, each genre emphasizes one of the fundamental elements of fiction: plot, character, setting, style, or theme.

For example, many genres are based upon the fundamental element of setting.

- Historical fiction: A setting that focuses on a particular time and place in the past.
- Science fiction: A setting that includes a futuristic world or universe.
- Fantasy: A setting that includes a magical or supernatural world.

Some genres focus on the fundamental element of character.

- Romance: Characters with a potentially loving relationship.
- Young adult: An adolescent character.

Some genres focus on the fundamental element of plot.

- Coming of age: Self-discovery as an adolescent matures.
- Mysteries: Efforts to solve a crime.
- Thriller: Preventing a disaster.
- Horror: Dealing with something scary.

Some genres focus on the fundamental element of style.

- Literary fiction: Style focused on how the fiction is presented.
- Postmodern fiction: Style focused on reminding readers that they are reading a work of fiction.

Some genres focus on the fundamental element of theme.

- Fable: A narration intended to enforce a useful truth, especially one in which animals speak and act like human beings.[3]
- Parable: A usually short fictitious story that illustrates a moral attitude or a religious principle.[4]
- Satire: A literary work holding up human vices and follies to ridicule or scorn, sometimes with an intent to bring about improvement.[5]

Within each category of fiction may be one or more *subgenres* emphasizing particular aspects of that group.

- Paranormal romance: Fiction focused on potentially romantic characters with extrasensory capabilities.
- Westerns: Historical fiction set in the American frontier with plots that pit characters struggling to address the challenges particular to that milieu.
- Medical thrillers: Fiction focused on preventing a healthcare disaster.

Some works of fiction don't fit neatly into any genre or subgenre. This may present a challenge for marketing a novel, from deciding how to describe the story to determining which shelf to place it on in a bookstore or which category best suits it in an online bookstore. For example, Delia Owens' *Where the Crawdads Sing* includes elements of survival, coming of age, romance, historical fiction, and murder mystery, but I wouldn't classify the novel in any of those genres.

Determining which genre best fits a work of fiction is largely a matter of identifying the story's dominant fundamental theme.

TAKEAWAYS

- The term *genre* refers to works of fiction that have one or more themes in common.
- The word *genre* means category.[6]
- Each genre emphasizes one of the fundamental elements of fiction: plot, character, setting, style, or theme.
- Within each category of fiction may be one or more *subgenres* emphasizing particular aspects of that group.
- Some works of fiction don't fit neatly into any genre or subgenre.

The next three chapters address message themes.

6

MESSAGE THEMES, PART 1— FICTION-WRITING MODES

As outlined in a previous chapter, plot, character, setting, and style each have their own themes, but what about the fifth element, theme? What are the "theme themes" that apply to that fundamental element, and what do we call them?

Theme is the *why* of fiction,[1] but what does that really mean? The *why* of a work of fiction can best be explained from the perspective of the author and may be expressed in the form of a simple question. What was the author trying to accomplish? Why did the author write the story? What point was the author making? The *point* may be any concept—an idea, an argument, a doctrine, a fact, an allegation. I believe the right word that encapsulates all these concepts is *message*,[2] and that means that "theme themes" may be appropriately categorized as *message themes*. John Gardner appears to support this concept when he wrote, "The writer speaks, first, to clarify in his own mind what he thinks and feels and, second, to make that clear to somebody else, on the assumption that the reader has sometimes felt, or can now be encouraged to feel the same."[3]

Authors have three means by which to communicate a message: (1) fiction-writing modes, (2) symbols, and (3) allegory. Fiction-writing modes will be covered in this chapter, while symbols and allegory will be addressed later.

FICTION-WRITING MODES

Kristin Hannah, in *The Four Winds*, communicates a message when she quotes farmer and poet Wendell Berry: "To damage the earth is to damage your children."[4] In this situation, the author uses the expository device of quoting a poem to express a message, but that same message may be presented in any of the eleven fiction-writing modes,[5] as shown below.

- DESCRIPTION: A massive, dark cloud of dust stormed toward them, as if nature were saying, "To damage the earth is to damage your children."
- ACTION: Elsa read from a poem by Wendell Berry, "To damage the earth is to damage your children," then gently closed the book.
- NARRATION: To damage the earth is to damage your children.
- CONVERSATION (dialogue): Elsa Wolcott quoted Wendell Berry, "To damage the earth is to damage your children."

- EXPOSITION: The quote, "To damage the earth is to damage your children," was written by poet Wendell Berry.
- SUMMARIZATION: The Dust Bowl of the Great Plains in the 1930s was nature's way of saying that "To damage the earth is to damage your children," referring to deep-plowing practices that left the soil vulnerable to drought and high winds.
- INTROSPECTION: Elsa realized that to damage the earth is to damage your children.
- SENSATION: Elsa woke with a start, her mouth and nose filled with dust. She gagged, sneezed, and coughed. Tasting muddy saliva, she rushed to her son's room, recalling the words, "To damage the earth is to damage your children."
- TRANSITION: As the evening light faded, Elsa read a line of poetry, "To damage the earth is to damage your children." Too tired to ponder such sentiments, she closed her eyes and fell asleep.
- EMOTION: Elsa blinked her tear-filled eyes and read the line again. "To damage the earth is to damage your children." She closed the book and sobbed.
- RECOLLECTION: Elsa recalled a line from a poem by Wendell Berry, "To damage the earth is to damage your children."

The examples above quote a poem, but examples of using fiction-writing modes to communicate a message abound in bestselling novels.

- Narration from *Lessons in Chemistry* by Bonnie Garmus: "The real issue with these people, besides the occasional hygiene challenge, was that they always seemed to embrace failure as a positive outcome."[6]
- Dialogue from *One Italian Summer* by Rebecca Serle: "'I don't think bad action makes you a bad person. I think life is far more complicated than that, and it's reductive to think otherwise.'"[7]
- Introspection from *It Ends With Us* by Colleen Hoover: "Just because someone hurts you doesn't mean you can simply stop loving them. It's not a person's actions that hurt the most. It's the love. If there was no love attached to the action, the pain would be a little easier to bear."[8]

In the novels I studied while I wrote this book, fiction-writing modes were a common means of communicating whatever message the writer desired.

TAKEAWAYS

- The *message* of a work of fiction may represent any concept—an idea, an argument, a doctrine, a fact, an allegation.
- The themes of the fundamental element of theme may be categorized as *message themes*.
- Authors have three means by which to communicate a message: (1) fiction-writing modes, (2) symbols, and (3) allegory.
- In written fiction, a message may be expressed in any of the eleven fiction-writing modes (presented here in the

order of the anagram DANCE SISTER): description, action, narration, conversation (dialogue), exposition, summary, introspection, sensation, transition, emotion, and recollection.

The next two chapters address symbols and allegory.

7

MESSAGE THEMES, PART 2—SYMBOLS

Advice about symbols ranges from use them to ignore them. "In fiction," according to Leonard Bishop's *Dare to Be a Great Writer*, "a *symbol* is any object, character, place, gesture, color, smell, etc., that carries meaning, not only for what it is but also for what it implies."[1] As stated by Donald Maass, in *Writing the Breakout Novel*, symbols "pack a powerful lot of meaning in a small package."[2] Noah Lukeman notes that symbols "speak to the reader's subconscious" and "often resonate with us at some deep level."[3]

CATEGORIES OF SYMBOLS

Raymond Obstfeld, in *Fiction First Aid*, says, "Symbols fall into two categories: universal symbols and situational symbols.[4] A *universal symbol* is any object, that conveys two meanings: (1) what it is in itself and (2) what tradition has caused it to suggest. ... The writer describes only the literal object; the reader brings into that description a deeper level of suggestion."[5]

Obstfeld identified five examples of universal symbols.[6]

1. Title—which may reference another literary work whose theme is familiar. For example, John Steinbeck's *East of Eden*,[7] which alludes to the Bible.
2. Homage plot—which openly uses the same plot as a famous story or myth to signal similarity between this story and the one being used. For example, *O Brother Where Art Thou*, which parallels *Sullivan's Travels*.[8]
3. Character names—which refer to others, thereby implying a connection. Sometimes names are direct, sometimes variations of the original. For example, Chris and Jesse vs Jesus Christ, Biblical names, or those from Greek and Roman mythology.[9]
4. Objects—for example, eyeglasses may be used as a symbol to show universal conflict about a character who is unable, or refuses, to see her situation and must, therefore, suffer the consequences.[10]
5. Setting—for example, hospitals, libraries, universities, scientific labs, and government buildings are often symbols of humanity's accumulated knowledge or the impotence of that knowledge.[11]

Non-universal symbols, which Obstfeld describes as *situational symbols*,[12] "are more personal and derive meaning from the context of a particular scene. They might hold no significance, or an entirely different one, in another scene."[13] As an example of a situational symbol, Bishop provides "a discarded scarf, a bone-china teacup with a broken handle. These objects require explanation. Because they do not carry 'universal suggestions;' they must be further explained." Kristin Hannah's *The Four Winds* features a U.S. penny portrayed as a symbol of hope for an immigrant family, but in another novel, a penny would probably just be a penny.

In fiction, symbols may be either universal or situational or both, depending on the circumstances. A train is a universal symbol of forward movement, but *The Girl on the Train* features a commuter train, which is a situational symbol that takes people back and forth in an endless cycle. The view from the train is a series of snapshots of scenery as the train rolls past, paralleling the main character's fragmented, alcohol-fogged memory.

USING SYMBOLS

My study of books about the craft of writing fiction reveals a broad range of advice for authors regarding the use of symbols, including (1) create and develop symbols, (2) avoid overuse and underuse of symbols, and (3) ignore symbols.

Create And Develop Symbols

According to Raymond Obstfeld, "Symbols and other thematic elements contribute greatly to a story's depth and allow readers to draw new meanings and interpretations from it even after repeated readings."[14] He adds, "Symbolism is a shorthand method for a writer to signal to the reader what the universal conflict, or theme, is."[15]

Leonard Bishop noted, "Writers should take advantage of the meanings contained within universal symbols. Universal symbols not only establish a setting, but also save on tedious descriptions. [For example], a flag is a tailored, colored piece of cloth. But a flag also suggests a particular nation. Bars across a window are used to prevent entry or exit through that window, but bars across a window also suggest the existence of a prison."[16]

Underuse Of Symbols

In *Fiction First Aid*, Obstfeld notes that if writers ignore symbols completely they are, "forsaking good opportunities to imbue stories with nuance and texture."[17]

Overuse Of Symbols

As stated by Leonard Bishop, "When symbols are forced into the work, they are either intrusive or amateurish."[18] Obstfeld agrees: overbearing use of symbols "trot them center stage as the concert percussionist crashes the cymbals—just to make sure you noticed."[19] If the symbols are center stage, readers may feel intellectually insulted and cease to take the writing seriously.[20] Bishop says, "The effectiveness of a symbol depends upon how subtly the writer leads the reader into discerning the undercurrent of its meaning."[21]

Regarding works that push for profundity, in 2003 Noah Lukeman wrote that many contemporary literary works emerging from MFA programs and published in literary journals prioritize well-crafted prose over a strong plot. The assumption often being that meticulous writing alone suffices, relegating plot to a secondary role. Lacking a compelling plot, these writers attempt to compensate through techniques like minimalism, symbolism, or metaphor, aiming to convey a deeper meaning that may not genuinely exist. This often results in unresolved paragraphs and chapters, hinting at a profound truth that remains elusive. True profundity arises from well-developed characters and engaging circumstances, not from attempts to impose meaning. If these writers prioritized a suspenseful plot, the quest for forced profundity might become unnecessary.[22]

Repetition

Repetition is an effective technique for communicating a message. According to John Gardner in *Moral Fiction*, "In art repetition is always a signal, intentional or not."[23] A *motif* is a distinctive recurring feature, such as a word, a phrase, or an object, that supports another aspect of a work of fiction.

According to Donald Maass, "Probably the most effective pattern to follow is that of a single symbol that recurs. Deployment of multiple symbols is possible too, of course, but what kind of power would J.R.R. Tolkien's *Lord of the Rings* have had if Frodo's quest had centered not only on a ring, but also on a sword, a comb, and a sack of flour?"[24]

Effectiveness Of Symbols

Leonard Bishop notes that "all symbols are subjectively interpretive. They are quixotic, untrustworthy. They are scented with formalism. Use them wisely or they will be smelled out and will fail."[25]

Donald Maass offers the following advice: "Evoking symbols is often a matter of making use of what is already there. If a symbol would otherwise naturally occur in a story, use it. It will not feel stagy. In fact, many readers may not consciously notice it."[26]

Ignore Symbols

Perhaps the best advice to writers regarding the use of symbols is from Leonard Bishop: "Be wary of using symbolism. ... If you believe you need a symbol to add undercurrents of meaning, then trust that your intentions have already produced them. This is not mystical or romantic. Symbols are all part of the content you are writing. What you emphasize and continue (like a thread through a tapestry) turns into the symbolic.[27]

TAKEAWAYS

- "In fiction, a *symbol* is any object, character, place, gesture, color, smell, etc., that carries meaning, not only for what it is, but also for what it implies."[28]
- "Symbols fall into two categories: universal symbols and situational symbols."[29]

- Five examples of universal symbols: titles, homage plot, character names, objects, and setting.[30]
- "Symbols and other thematic elements contribute greatly to a story's depth and allow readers to draw new meanings and interpretations from it even after repeated readings."[31]
- "In art repetition is always a signal, intentional or not."[32]
- A *motif* is a distinctive recurring feature, such as a word, a phrase, or an object, that supports another aspect of a work of fiction.
- Symbols are subjectively interpretive, quixotic, and untrustworthy, so use them wisely or they will fail.[33]
- "Symbols are all part of the content you are writing. What you emphasize and continue turns into the symbolic."[34]

The next chapter addresses how to let the words and actions of characters communicate a message through allegory.

8

MESSAGE THEMES, PART 3— ALLEGORY

Fiction may be viewed as the "expression by means of symbolic fictional figures and actions of truths or generalizations about human existence," which happens to be the definition of *allegory*.[1] Stated differently, the characters, events, setting, and style of written fiction come together in a manner that creates an underlying message about the nature of mankind.

Not all fiction includes allegory: for example, (1) a series of events that doesn't result in a resolution may be a mere *chronicle of events*; (2) a portrayal of a character may amount to nothing more than a *characterization*; (3) a description of place and time may only add up to a *travelogue*, and (4) an illustration of a particular manner of writing may represent only a *demonstration* of style. Other examples include segments of writing that are nothing more than a slice of life or a case study. Each of these examples generates little, if any, allegorical meaning. To fully understand the craft of writing fiction, we need to know how the fundamental elements combine to create something that is greater than the sum of its parts: a story.

More than just fundamental elements are needed to create a story. In *Third-Person Possessed*, I define a *story* as "a work of writing that dramatizes a character's attempts to achieve a goal."[2] Let me break this definition down. *A work of writing* clarifies what is being defined, as opposed to stage plays and screenplays and verbal storytelling. *Dramatizes* addresses the style of the writing by suggesting that the intent is to create reader interest, to entertain, to generate an emotional reaction. *A character* reflects the concept that without a character, there is no story. *Attempts to achieve a goal* reflect *plot*, in which the character must have an objective and must make multiple attempts to achieve it.[3]

This definition of *story* includes reference to style, character, and plot, but it doesn't mention setting and theme. The definition could certainly be expanded to include those elements, but doing so isn't necessary. A story cannot exist without a setting (a place and time), so by default it's there, with no need to include it in the definition. Likewise, the telling of a story automatically generates a theme as the character strives to attain his goal, so including theme in the definition of a story is also unnecessary. Every story, by its nature, has a built-in setting and theme.[4]

Story is a lot like cake. The process of baking a cake causes a chemical reaction that melds flour, eggs, sugar, etc. into something new (cake) in which the ingredients are no longer easily distinguishable or separable. Likewise, the process of developing a story creates a product in which events, character, setting, theme, and style become more difficult to distinguish and separate. In effect, plot, character, setting, theme, and style get "baked into the cake" of a story.[5]

That doesn't mean that the fundamental elements are unrecognizable after the story is written. Just as we can identify some ingredients of cake after it's baked (sugar, for example), we can still identify plot, character, setting, style, and theme in story. That's important because plot (particularly the ending) offers us the single best clue to the message of a story.

The beginning of a story establishes the *story question*: "Will the main character be able to achieve his or her goal?" The middle of the story shows the character attempting to achieve his or her goal. The end of a story answers the story question of whether or not the character is successful in achieving the goal. That answer creates allegory, i.e., the *story message*.

Aristotle recognized this concept over two thousand years ago when he divided stories into two types: (1) those in which the story goal is achieved and (2) those in which the story goal is not achieved. Aristotle called the first category of stories *comedy* and the second *tragedy*.[6] Today, those categories are commonly referred to as (1) stories with a happy ending and (2) stories with a sad ending.

Aristotle deserves credit for identifying two broad story themes:

1. Persistence in achieving a goal leads to success, which results in a comedy, including a happy ending.
2. Even if you persist in your effort to achieve a goal, you may fail, which results in a tragedy, including a sad ending.

More recently, in *Story*, Robert McKee expanded and renamed these concepts into three categories:[7]

1. *Idealistic*, up-ending stories "expressing the optimism, hopes, and dreams of mankind, a positively charged vision of the human spirit; life as we wish it to be."[8]
2. *Pessimistic*, down-ending stories "expressing our cynicism, our sense of loss and misfortune, a negatively charged vision of civilization's decline, of humanity's dark dimensions; life as we dread it to be but know it so often is."[9]
3. *Ironic*, up/down-ending stories "expressing our sense of the complex, dual nature of existence, a simultaneously charged positive and negative vision (a twist which wrenches an outcome that is not neatly positive or negative); life at its most complete and realistic."[10]

For the sake of brevity and clarity, I refer to these types of tales —and the messages they suggest—as (1) optimistic, (2) pessimistic, and (3) ironic. Because these concepts are all-encompassing, I believe that any work of fiction that rises to the level of a story also falls into one of these three categories.

I also note that tales with an ironic ending may be divided into two groups.

1. Optimistic with an ironic twist: The character achieves his goal, or part of it, but with an additional unexpected consequence. McKee offers an example of this type of theme: "If you cling to your obsession, your ruthless pursuit will achieve your desire, then destroy you."[11] This message could be called "Losing by winning" or "Success, but ..." Examples of this type of story abound, but one example (I won't spoil the ending for you), is Lisa Gardner's *One Step Too Far*, in which the main character solves a missing-person case by revealing the culprit to be (ironically) someone you would least suspect.
2. Pessimistic with an ironic twist: The character fails to achieve his goal but with an additional unexpected consequence. McKee offers an example of this type of story: "The compulsive pursuit of contemporary values —success, fortune, fame, sex, power—will destroy you, but if you see this truth in time and throw away your obsession, you can redeem yourself."[12] This message may also be described as "winning by losing"[13] or "failure, but ..." For example, in John Grisham's *A Time for Mercy*, the main character fails to achieve a "not guilty" verdict for his young client, but he does manage

to help his client avoid the death sentence—at least temporarily.

To illustrate these concepts, let's rethink one of the most resonating works of fiction ever told: William Shakespeare's play *Romeo and Juliet*. This story features the master plot of forbidden love: lovers who belong to violently rival tribes. Shakespeare could have structured the story differently in at least four ways:

- An optimistic ending, in which Romeo and Juliet, against all odds, somehow find happiness together.
- A pessimistic ending, in which Romeo and Juliet, because of the formidable opposition they face, are forced to break off their relationship and go their separate ways.
- An optimistic ending with an ironic twist, in which Romeo and Juliet find happiness together but then one of them dies.
- A pessimistic ending with an ironic twist, in which Romeo and Juliet are forced to give each other up but then each find love in the arms of another and live happily ever after.

Each of these alternative endings has the potential to be an interesting story, but Shakespeare opted for another approach, an optimistic ending (Romeo and Juliet successfully marry) with an ironic double twist, in which Romeo and Juliet each think the other is dead and take their own life.

Based on the above, the process of discovering a story's message begins by categorizing the resolution as either optimistic, pessimistic, or ironic, and if applicable, whether the resolution is optimistic with an ironic twist or pessimistic with an ironic twist.

The simplest of stories (those with a single plot) may be easily categorized as either optimistic, pessimistic, or ironic:

- If the focal character achieves his goal, the message is optimistic.
- If the focal character fails, the message is pessimistic.
- If the focal character is successful but with unexpected consequences, the message is optimistic with an ironic twist.
- If the focal character fails but with unexpected consequences, the message is pessimistic with an ironic twist.

A *simple story* includes only one plot. Novels often have more than one plot, and each plot creates its own allegory, or message. In a simple plot, the main character faces either (1) external obstacles or (2) internal obstacles. But many stories are told with two plots: an external plot *and* an internal plot. Frequently, this pairing dramatizes the character's attempts to overcome *external* obstacles while also struggling to address *internal* issues that hinder her chances of achieving her external goal. This dramatization of both an external and an internal plot creates a more complicated and interesting story.

Any story may be made more complex by adding parallel plots and subplots. I define *parallel plots* as two or more plots that more or less run the whole length of the work of fiction. I define a *main plot* as the most significant plot that runs the entire length of the story. I define a *subplot* as a plot that runs for less than the whole length of the work of fiction.

Plots and subplots may involve either external or internal obstacles. These plots may be viewed as separate parts of the work or viewed in combination as either complex or compound. I define a *complex story* as one that includes one or more subplots, for example, an external plot and an internal subplot. I define a *compound story* as having two or more plots (either internal or external) that run the whole length of the work of fiction. A *complex, compound story* would then include two or more plots (either internal or external) that run the whole length of the work of fiction *and* at least one subplot (external or internal).

A work of fiction may have a message for each plot, whether that plot is external or internal, a parallel plot, or a subplot. The message for each plot may be unrelated to the message for the other plots, or those messages may complement or contrast with each other, adding another layer of richness to the work as a whole. An example of a story with a complex plot is Laura Dave's *The Last Thing He Told Me* (Spoiler alert).

In the inciting incident Hannah Hall receives a handwritten note from Owen Michaels, her husband of one year: *Protect her*. Hannah correctly assumes the "her" in the note refers to Owen's sixteen-year-old daughter, but the message creates the main plot question: Somehow, she must protect Bailey. That question is soon joined by others that form multiple subplots: Protect Bailey from what and why? Where is Owen? Why has he disappeared?

When Owen's boss is arrested by the FBI, other questions arise: Who, really, is Owen? Is he also a criminal? In addition to these mysteries, Hannah also struggles internally, wondering if Bailey will ever accept her as a friend, much less a stepmother. And Hannah wonders whether she is being a steadfast spouse or just being played as a fool.

Working together to solve these mysteries, Hannah and Bailey grow closer, but once Hannah discovers why Owen disappeared and who he really is, she faces new questions: how can she save Owen's life, Bailey's, and her own? In the end, Hannah is successful in protecting Bailey, Owen, and herself, but at such crushing cost that I classify this as an optimistic story with an ironic twist.

In recent chapters we have reviewed three means by which writers communicate a message: (1) fiction-writing modes, (2) symbols, and (3) allegory. Although these means were presented separately here, they are commonly used together in a work of fiction.

TAKEAWAYS

- *Allegory* is the use of symbolic figures and actions to express truths or generalizations about human conduct or experience.[14] Stated differently, the characters,

events, setting, and style of written fiction come together in a manner that creates an underlying message about the nature of mankind.
- Not all works of fiction include allegory. Examples include a chronicle of events, a characterization, a travelogue, a demonstration of style, a slice of life, or a case study.
- A *story* is "a work of writing that dramatizes a character's attempts to achieve a goal."
- Any work of fiction that rises to the level of a story may be categorized by the type of message it suggests—optimistic, pessimistic, or ironic.
- Ironic stories may be classified as either (1) optimistic with unexpected consequences or (2) pessimistic with unexpected consequences.
- A *simple story* includes only one plot.
- *Parallel plots* include two or more plots that run more or less the whole length of the work of fiction.
- The *main plot* is the most significant plot that runs the entire length of the story.
- A *complex story* is one that includes one or more subplots.
- A *compound story* is one that includes two or more plots (either internal or external) that run the whole length of the work of fiction.
- A *complex, compound story* includes two or more plots and at least one subplot.

The next chapter addresses message and propaganda.

9

MESSAGE VS. PROPAGANDA

The notion that authors intentionally include a message in a story brings to mind an emotion-laden word in fiction writing: propaganda. Its inclusion in phrases like *religious propaganda, political propaganda*, and *Nazi propaganda* gives it a negative connotation. Labeling a work of fiction as propaganda is considered criticism, as in "Them's fighting words." Because the word propaganda may stimulate such an emotional reaction, we need to thoroughly understand what it is and what it isn't, so we may handle it appropriately.

CONNOTATION AND DENOTATION

Clearly, the word propaganda has a negative connotation. John Gardner's *On Moral Fiction* refers to "The subversion of art to the purposes of propaganda."[1] In fiction writing, other words and phrases associated with propaganda include moralizing, preaching, and writing with an agenda. Today, *propa-*

ganda is often considered "denoting ideas or information that are of questionable accuracy as a means of advancing a cause."[2]

To fully understand propaganda, we must look deeper. Let's start with a clear definition, the word's *denotation*. According to *Webster's Third International Dictionary*, *propaganda* is defined as "doctrines, ideas, arguments, facts, or allegations spread by deliberate effort through any medium of communication in order to further one's cause or to damage an opposing cause."[3] That's a long definition, so let's break it down and simplify it for use in the context of written fiction.

- *Doctrines, ideas, arguments, facts, or allegations* may be summarized simply as "a message."
- Unless the author writes solely for his own consumption, all fiction is *spread by deliberate effort*, so we may delete that phrase from the definition.
- Written fiction is distributed as either hard copies or digital media, so including *through any medium of communication* in the definition is unnecessary for our purposes.
- The phrase *in order to further one's cause or to damage an opposing cause* may be eliminated from the definition if we assume that the purpose of any message included in written fiction is to further a cause or to damage one. Why else would a message be included?

Based on this reasoning, I believe that in the context of written fiction, the word *propaganda* may be viewed as synonymous with *message*, any distinction being without meaningful difference.

PRAISE FOR PROPAGANDA

Not everything written about propaganda is negative. John Gardner's *On Moral Fiction* notes that "some good and '"serious'" fiction is merely first-class propaganda."[4] He also wrote, "I agree with Tolstoy that the highest purpose of art is to make people good by choice."[5] Gardner goes on to state that moral art often showcases virtuous characters in stories, movies, and plays, providing us with inspiration and strength in our own battles against chaos and wrongdoing.[6]

QUALITIES OF MESSAGE

A message may have various qualities: (1) intentionality, (2) truthfulness, (3) innocuousness, (4) obtrusiveness, (5) explicitness, (6) implicitness, (7) effectiveness, (8) originality, (9) profundity, and (10) resonance, each of which will be addressed in the following paragraphs.

Intentionality

The author may include a message in a story in two ways: intentionally or unintentionally. How, you might ask, could an author include a message without realizing he or she is doing so? All of us have a personal *worldview*, how we perceive the way things work—or should work. Unless an author intentionally writes a story that contrasts with his or her own worldview, the author is likely to subconsciously (unintentionally) include a message that reflects his personal views. That's human nature.

Nancy Kress, in *Dynamic Characters*, put it this way: "It's impossible to write a story—or even a few significant paragraphs—without implying a worldview. This is because the writer has *always* chosen to include some events and some details and to leave others out. Furthermore, the writer has—wittingly or not—chosen a *tone* in which to present those details, and that tone, too, implies a worldview."[7]

Rather than spend effort assessing the intentions of authors, I prefer to assume that authors are in control of what they write and that any message in a story was developed by the author, either consciously or subconsciously, because that message conforms to the author's beliefs, her worldview. Authors should know what they are doing at all times, rather than leaving aspects of their work to be left to their subconscious or to chance. Even if an author didn't intend to include the message, how can readers determine that? If the story has a message, the author put it there; it's irrelevant whether the message was consciously or subconsciously included by the author.

Truthfulness

When I googled *antonym of propaganda*, the most prominent word that popped up was *truth*. As already shown, the dictionary definition of propaganda does not address the truthfulness of a message. The definition is neutral on this subject. Whether or not you consider a message to be propaganda, it may be truthful—or not—or anywhere in between.

Innocuousness

As with truthfulness, the dictionary definition of propaganda does not address whether the message is *nocuous*, "likely to cause injury: harmful, damaging."[8] A message may range in nocuousness from nocuous to *innocuous*, which is defined as (1) "producing no ill effect, (2) not likely to arouse animus or give offense, or (3) not likely to arouse strong feelings."[9] One reader may label a message as propaganda while another may consider the same message to be "telling it like it is." One person's blatant propaganda may be another person's cherished wisdom. It's subjective, as in the "eye of the beholder" or "I'll recognize it when I see it."

Innocuous messages abound in fiction: justice prevails, love conquers all, persistence is rewarded, to name just a few. On the other end of the spectrum, a message promoting genocide, slavery, or sexual abuse would likely receive universal condemnation as nocuous. Between these two extremes is a vast pool of issues about which many people disagree, a portion of which believe very strongly one way, and another portion who just as strongly believe the opposite. A message promoting one side of an issue is likely to be perceived as nocuous propaganda by one group, while the other group perceives the message as affirming their beliefs.

Obtrusiveness

A message may be as obtrusive as the one in Aesop's Fables "The Boy Who Cried Wolf," the whole purpose of which is to warn that spreading a false alarm may cost you your life. Or a message may be so unobtrusive that you must look closely to find it.

One type of obtrusive message is what I call an *opinion dump*, where the author inserts a passage of writing to communicate his or her own views. Sometimes such a message is disguised with the fiction-writing modes of dialogue or introspection, but it may also come directly from the author as narration. Rather than provide an example, I'll trust that you'll recognize an opinion dump when you read one.

Explicitness

The definition of *explicit* is "characterized by full, clear expression; being without vagueness or ambiguity, leaving nothing implied, unequivocal."[10] Other terms for explicit include *stated* and *spelled out*. When a story message is presented through the fiction-writing mode of narration, that message is explicit, having been expressed by the author directly to the reader. Likewise, the message is explicit if it is expressed as a character's dialogue or thoughts, using the fiction-writing modes of conversation or introspection.

Lessons in Chemistry by Bonnie Garmus, which is set in the 1960s, is filled with explicit messages presented through fiction-writing modes.

- NARRATION: "Elizabeth Zott held grudges too. Except her grudges were mainly reserved for a patriarchal society founded on the idea that women were less."[11]
- INTROSPECTION: "Most of the women she'd met in college claimed they were only there to get their MRS. It was disconcerting, as if they'd all drunk something that had rendered them temporarily insane."[12]
- DIALOGUE: "'One thing I've learned, Calvin: people will always yearn for a simple solution to their complicated problems.'"[13]

Implicitness

The opposite of explicit is *implicit*, which is "involved in the nature or essence of something though not revealed, expressed, or developed."[14] Other terms for *implicit* include *tacit* and *subtext*. When a message emerges from allegory, that message is implicit, having arisen from the action and words of the characters, without actually stating the message.

A story may include both explicit messages and implicit messages. Kristin Hannah's *The Four Winds* includes plenty of allegory, but the author also uses various fiction-writing modes to communicate message explicitly. For example, "Regret reemerges at the oddest moments."[15] "Hope is a coin I carry, given to me by a woman I will always love, and I hold it now as I journey west, part of a new generation of seekers."[16] These are examples of an author explicitly expressing a message, spelling it out for us.

Effectiveness

Effectiveness is the degree to which the presentation of a message is successful in producing the author's intended result. Effectiveness ranges from extremely effective to ineffective, and the difference is a result of the skill with which the writer makes his or her presentation.

"The Boy Who Cried Wolf" has an obtrusive message, but it is also very effective. Countless popular novels in all genres effectively affirm that "persistence pays" as a couple finds love, justice prevails, or the heroine saves the day.

As stated by Donald Maass, "There are ways to make an unpopular point compelling, and there are ways to make it repellant. A novelist hoping to break out will, naturally enough, shoot for the former effect."[17]

Originality

According to Donald Maass, "Few novelists want to say exactly what has been said before. Most would prefer to be visionary."[18] But one could argue that there are no new messages, only timeworn variations of the same old messages imitated time and again over the centuries. Disparaging terms for imitative or derivative messages include *trope*, *cliché*, *tired*, and *timeworn*. In the words of John Gardner, "The great artist, whatever the form he chooses, breaks through the limited reality around him and makes a new one."[19]

Some stories recast even the oldest messages with a new approach or angle. Positive terms for such themes may include *fresh, innovative,* or *imaginative.* An example of this is Jodi Picoult's *Wish You Were Here,* in which she pairs the message that time may be multidimensional (a common theme in science fiction) with a near-death Covid-epidemic experience. Bonnie Garmus's *Lessons in Chemistry* is an entertaining look at the painful subject of sex discrimination. Both of these novels are examples of how time changes the perspective of readers, offering authors opportunities to explore themes in new ways.

Profundity

A message may be *profound*,[20] having intellectual depth going thoroughly and penetratingly into a problem, possessing knowledge and insight.[21] Or a message may range in profoundness down to a level that may be considered superficial or intellectually shallow. For example, regardless of genre, a novel may be thoroughly entertaining but may include only superficial meaning about the nature of mankind. On the other end of the spectrum is fiction with such profound meaning that it may challenge a reader's deepest beliefs. For example, *The Da Vinci Code* by Dan Brown challenges the traditional perception of the Holy Grail.

Resonance

Some messages echo back, or *resonate,* and may stick with us for quite a while. Donald Maass in *Writing the Breakout Novel* notes the impact of effectively integrating an internal conflict with the external plot in a story. He suggests that if an author skillfully develops a moral conflict, aligning its climax with the plot's climax, the likely result is a memorable message.[22]

For mature adults such as myself, who recall "The Boy Who Cried Wolf" from childhood, the story has long-term resonance, while hundreds of other titles are long forgotten.

UBIQUITOUS PROPAGANDA

If every work of fiction that rises to the level of a story includes a message, and *message* is synonymous with *propaganda*, then propaganda is ubiquitous in fiction. It's not *if* a work of fiction includes a message, but *where* it is. If it's a story, a message is there, else it wouldn't be a story. And that's a good thing because the vast majority of fiction presents a message that is beneficial to mankind. I suspect that most messages reflect a wholesome worldview in the author's mind. How many novels are you aware of that promote genocide, slavery, or sexual abuse? I can't think of any.

I find the concept that *propaganda* and *message* are synonymous makes the analysis of fiction more efficient. I no longer need to go through the uncomfortable mental process of determining *whether* propaganda is in a work of fiction; I just assume all stories include a message, and I keep looking until I find it. Improved understanding of messages enables us to identify them in our own work and in the work of others and then to objectively evaluate them.

ALTERNATIVES TO PROPAGANDA

Since the word propaganda has a negative connotation, I recommend that we not use it in the context of written fiction except when we intend it as criticism. For the remainder of this book, I intend to avoid the use of propaganda when I can. In situations where I wish to call attention to a message for which the author is clearly developing a message to "further one's cause or to damage an opposing cause," I'll use sanitized alternatives such as *advancing or promoting a message, bolstering an objective*, or *championing a point of view*. If we avoid the word propaganda, we can analyze messaging in stories without the related emotional baggage.

OTHER CONSIDERATIONS

Including a message in a work of fiction has potential risks and rewards, and we need to assess the pros and cons of each. Is the message likely to be affirmative for the readers and thus likely to be welcomed by them? Or is the message more likely to be perceived with hostility? Are parents, teachers, and librarians likely to perceive the message as wholesome for young people? How are editors and publishers likely to react? Who and how many people will be offended by the message? If a significant portion of your project's potential readers are put off by the messages in your novel, online book reviews will reflect that, as will sales.

Promoting a message may exact a cost on the author. For example, the "Note from the Author" section of Colleen Hoover's *It*

Ends with Us includes the following: "In the past, I've always said I write for entertainment purposes only. I don't write to educate, persuade, or inform. This book is different."[23] The novel portrays the main character in a domestic-abuse relationship, and Hoover reveals how uncomfortable she felt while writing the manuscript. Clearly, championing a cause is not for every writer. Colleen Hoover pulls it off skillfully, building awareness of a terrible problem, and reaping the rewards in book sales. An author's decisions as to whether to champion a point of view and how to promote that message need to be carefully considered.

RESPONSIBILITY

The ability to write in a manner that influences readers intellectually is a powerful skill that may be used for the benefit of mankind or for its detriment. With power comes responsibility. As writers, teachers, and students of the craft of writing fiction, we have a responsibility to recognize messages and to understand them.

If we understand *message* and accept that the term isn't disparaging, then we can use that knowledge to more effectively recognize messages we support and those we disagree with. Understanding messages enables us, as authors, to improve the persuasiveness of our own writing, if we choose to use it.

As authors, we have an opportunity to develop messages that shed light on issues and offer solutions to problems. Writing fiction may be viewed as exercising social responsibility, a form of community service, hopefully making the world just a little better. Whether or not you choose to deliberately promote a message, more than likely your stories are already "telling it like it is," as you see it, consistent with your own worldview. Regardless of whether you choose to deliberately promote your views, other authors are doing so, either consciously or subconsciously, whether they admit it or not.

How do we promote messages that are wholesome? By writing about characters in challenging situations and how those characters address those issues. In other words, by doing our job of writing great stories.

TAKEAWAYS

- The word *propaganda* has a negative connotation and is often considered to mean "denoting ideas or information that are of questionable accuracy as a means of advancing a cause."[24]
- *Propaganda*'s definition, its *denotation* is "doctrines, ideas, arguments, facts, or allegations spread by deliberate effort through any medium of communication in order to further one's cause or to damage an opposing cause,"[25] which, in the context of written fiction, may be viewed as synonymous with *message*.
- Regardless of whether a message is labeled as propaganda, it may have various qualities: (1) intentionality, (2) truthfulness, (3) innocuousness, (4) obtrusiveness, (5) explicitness, (6) implicitness, (7)

effectiveness, (8) originality, (9) profundity, and (10) resonance.
- The author may include a message in a story in two ways: intentionally or unintentionally.
- Unless an author intentionally writes a story that contrasts with his or her own worldview, the author is likely to subconsciously include a message that reflects his personal views.
- It's irrelevant whether the message of a story was consciously or subconsciously included by the author.
- Whether or not a message is propaganda, it may be truthful—or not—or anywhere in between.
- A message may range from nocuous to innocuous.
- A message may be obtrusive or so unobtrusive that you must look closely to find it.
- An *opinion dump* is where an author inserts into the story a passage of writing to communicate his or her own views, sometimes thinly disguised with the fiction-writing modes of dialogue or introspection, or it may come directly from the author as narration.
- A message may be explicit, or it may be implicit.
- A message may be effective or not.
- One could argue that there are no new messages, only timeworn variations of the same old messages imitated time and again over the centuries.
- Disparaging terms for imitative or derivative messages include *trope, cliché, tired, and timeworn.*
- Some stories recast even the oldest messages with a new approach or angle, earning descriptions that include *fresh, innovative,* or *imaginative.*

- A message can range in profoundness down to a level that may be considered superficial or intellectually shallow.
- Some messages resonate, while others do not.
- If every work of fiction that rises to the level of a story includes a message, then the question is not *if* a work of fiction includes a message, but *what* it is.
- To avoid the negative emotional baggage of the word propaganda, use sanitized alternatives such as *advancing or promoting a message, bolstering an objective,* or *championing a point of view.*
- The ability to write in a manner that influences readers intellectually is a powerful skill that may be used for the benefit of mankind or for its detriment; with power comes responsibility.
- Understanding messages enables authors to improve the persuasiveness of their own writing if they choose to do so.
- Authors have an opportunity to develop messages that shed light on issues and offer solutions to problems, hopefully making the world just a little better.

The next chapter addresses strategies for message development.

HELP SHAPE A STORYTELLER'S JOURNEY

YOUR WORDS CAN INSPIRE GREATNESS

Every story we tell, every novel we write, is a step towards understanding ourselves and the world around us. It's like building a bridge between hearts and minds.

Imagine you could help others find their voice and guide them to tell stories that resonate and linger in the heart and mind of readers. What if a few words from you could be the nudge that propels a budding writer toward achieving his or her dream?

I have a question for you. Would you offer a helping hand to an aspiring writer, knowing your words could light that person's path? Picture this writer as eager, bright-eyed, brimming with stories yet untold, where you once were—at the beginning of a journey, seeking wisdom, craving guidance.

Years ago, I set out on a quest to decode the essence of impactful storytelling. My hope for *How to Write a Novel That Matters* is that it becomes a beacon for fiction writers everywhere. To do this, I need to reach every storyteller, every dreamer who puts pen to paper.

This is where you come in. Yes, the first thing most people notice about a book is its cover, but they also judge a book by its reviews. So, here's my heartfelt request on behalf of a writer you may never meet. Please consider writing a review for this book.

It's a simple act, taking less than a minute, but your words could be the key that unlocks another writer's potential. Your review might inspire a story that changes lives.

- Help a writer find his or her voice.
- Make someone's dream of writing a reality.
- Aid a storyteller in weaving tales that matter.

To share your thoughts and help a fellow writer, just follow these easy steps. It's quick. Just scan the QR code below to leave your review:

https://www.amazon.com/review/create-review/?asin=B0CV82FJT3

If you feel the joy of assisting another writer, then you're exactly the kind of person I wrote this book for. Welcome to our community of storytellers. You're now part of something bigger.

I'm thrilled to guide you through the journey of writing a novel that truly matters. So far, this book has addressed *what* matters in fiction. The upcoming chapters focus on *how* to write fiction that matters.

Thank you.
—Mike Klaassen

P.S. Remember, sharing knowledge is a gift that enriches both the giver and the receiver. If you think this book may assist another writer, teacher, or student of fiction, pass it along. Let's spread the wisdom and joy of storytelling.

10

STRATEGIES FOR MESSAGE DEVELOPMENT

I've identified eight strategies for developing a story's message: ignore, plan, discover, explore, choose, enhance, integrate, and retrofit. Some of these strategies may be used throughout the writing process; others are more appropriate during one or more of the five distinct message-development timeframes: (1) never, (2) before manuscript creation, (3) during first-draft creation, (4) during editing and revision, and (5) after manuscript creation. The remainder of this chapter addresses each of the message-development strategies and the timeframes in which those strategies are most appropriate.

IGNORE THE MESSAGE

One way to address messages is to just ignore them. According to Flannery O'Connor: "It takes every word in the story to say what the meaning is."[1] To which Brandi Reissenweber adds, "So don't get caught up in excavating message and holding it up to the light for inspection."[2]

A. B. Guthrie, Jr., in *A Field Guide to Writing Fiction*, wrote, "Every good story has a theme, recognized or not. Tell your story and don't worry. The theme lies in it, maybe to be discovered by critics, not by you. ... Themes are critics' concerns, not necessarily yours."[3]

I suspect quite a few successful authors share this laissez-faire attitude and simply don't worry about message at all. Edgar Allen Poe once wrote, "Most writers ... prefer having it understood that they compose by a species of fine frenzy—and ecstatic intuition."[4] Even writers who deliberately plan and execute other aspects of fiction, such as plot and characterization, may profess a lack of planning regarding the message of their story.

Whenever I learn of a successful author who disclaims any attempt to develop message, I think of what Peter Selgin admits in *By Cunning and Craft*: "We fiction writers don't always know what we're doing."[5] I believe that it is more accurate to say that authors who ignore message don't *consciously* address that concept. Successful message development for them may be a matter of instinct, or the development of message occurs subconsciously. Writers may address the message of a story consciously or subconsciously, or both.

No doubt some authors have a knack for developing the message of a story, and to them, the message just naturally grows from the stories they write. I also believe that what may seem a natural talent may actually be an amalgam of knowledge and common sense accumulated over a lifetime and that the brain draws on that expertise without the conscious effort of the writer.

If that's the case, then gaining a more thorough understanding of message and how it's developed can help an author's subconscious mind address the issue. More than likely, you selected this book because you are at least a little curious about message and learning how to improve it in your writing projects. The remainder of this chapter addresses the *conscious* development of message.

PLAN THE MESSAGE

The concept of planning a story goes back a long way. Consider the following words of Edgar Allan Poe: "It is my design to render it manifest that no point in its composition is referable either to accident or intuition—that the work proceeded step by step, to its completion, with the precision and rigid consequence of a mathematical problem."[6]

Deliberate message identification and development (i.e., planning) can start at the beginning of the story-development process. Message can even be the inspiration for the story: the acorn from which the entire project develops. Each of my three novels to date has a clear message:

- *The Brute*—Anger management can help you take charge of a life reeling out of control.

- *Cracks*—Rather than wasting your life yearning for something that will never materialize, learn to appreciate what you already have.
- *Backlash*—War can last longer, be vastly more expensive, and have very different consequences than imagined at the beginning.

Now that the novels are completed, I can see that each of the messages described above could have been the inspiration for the story, literally the first words scribbled on a scrap of paper, followed by ideas for character, plot, setting, and style.

Whether or not message is the original inspiration for your story, early in the planning process, you may have a message in mind, or at least a *preliminary message*, to use as a placeholder until a better one emerges. Once you have a working message as part of your story structure, you can then expand on the concept, planning your entire story with that message as an integral part. As described by Ronald B. Tobias in *Theme & Structure*, "Theme is your inertial guidance system. It directs your decisions about which path to take, which choice is right for the story and which choice isn't. As we write, we only start to understand the actual meaning of the work, but with theme, we actually structure the work on a *concept* that guides us from the start." [7]

Over the years, I've learned to use a story-planning process that includes the following steps.

1. Record preliminary thoughts regarding the fundamental elements of the proposed story: (1) plot, (2) character, (3) setting, (4) theme, and (5) style.
2. Write a one-sentence description for the story, working in the main character, the setting, the spark of a plot, and, if possible, a hint of the message.
3. Expand the one-sentence description to a paragraph with five sentences, each corresponding to a segment of the plot.
4. Expand the one-paragraph summary to a five-paragraph synopsis of the story, with each paragraph corresponding to a segment of the plot.
5. Expand the five-paragraph synopsis into an act-by-act, scene-by-scene outline of the story.
6. Use the outline of the story as a guide for writing the first draft.

The concept of using message as the primary guide to shaping a story was also championed by Edgar Allan Poe: "A skillful literary artist has constructed a tale. If wise, he has not fashioned his thoughts to accommodate his incidents; but having conceived, with deliberate care, a certain unique or single effect to be wrought out, he then invents such incidents—he then combines such events as may best aid him in establishing this preconceived effect."[8]

Writing is largely a matter of selection: what to include and what to exclude. In *By Cunning and Craft*, Peter Selgin connects selection to theme: "We must select and discriminate, and theme gives us the basis for doing so."[9]

DISCOVER THE MESSAGE

In the last century, authors of books about writing fiction have had a lot to say about the discovery of message. In 1978 John Gardner referred to "the process of discovery,"[10] and in 1997 Robert McKee stated that, "We rarely know where we are going; writing is discovery."[11] In 2002 Raymond Obstfeld wrote, "the act of writing is in fact the journey of discovering theme."[12] In 2008, James Scott Bell noted that "Some writers … have theme firmly in mind as they write. Others wait until they've finished the novel then look to see what theme has emerged."[13]

Regardless of whether you (1) ignore message at the beginning of your writing process, (2) begin your writing process with a specific message in mind, or (3) use a process somewhere in between, at any point along the way you may discover one or more messages of your tale, maybe even the one that epitomizes your story.

Ronald Tobias, in *Theme and Strategy* (1989), notes that theme develops during the course of the work. "We may think we know what our work is really about, but the experience of writing usually changes all our preconceived notions. … As you write, the horizons of your work will constantly open up."[14]

That doesn't mean that discovering the message of a story is easy. In *Fiction First Aid* (2002), Ray Obstfeld wrote, "Novels are never about what they are about; that is, there is always deeper, or more general, significance. ... And the job becomes one of understanding ... what is already written. That is finding the theme."[15]

Perhaps the most inciteful and helpful observation comes from Robert McKee in *Story* (1997), when he recommends that, to discover the message of a story, we look at how the plot ends, how the climax is resolved.[16] In the ending, we learn how the story question is answered, and from there we can look to determine the *why* of the outcome,[17] which reveals the story's message.

EXPLORE THE MESSAGE

The writing process may include considering and exploring[18] numerous messages. A reality of writing fiction is that, at any part of the writing process (from conception to final drafts), the author may realize that the story reflects a message that is not satisfactory to the author. James Scott Bell, in 2008, wrote that it's okay to change your mind about message.[19]

One of my writing projects is Klaassen's Classic Folktales, in which I retell fairy tales using today's storytelling techniques. Early in the process of reimagining "Jack and the Beanstalk," I determined that the messages of the traditional tale include *gullibility, greed, and theft are rewarded,* so one of my priorities was to rewrite the story with more noble messages. I faced similar challenges with "Hansel and Gretel," "The Frog Prince," and "Cinderella." For each of these tales, I brainstormed alternative messages that projected positive principles and then restructured the stories to support the new messages.

CHOOSE THE MESSAGE

The emergence of multiple message candidates for your story may seem frustrating, but this is a problem that also creates opportunity. Don't be surprised if the message that best matches your story is quite different from the one you identified earlier in the process.

"Selectivity—choosing what to include and what to omit in a novel—is an important part of a writer's work."[20] Few choices a writer makes have as much impact on a story as the writer's choice of messages.

ENHANCE THE MESSAGE

Once you have identified the message of your story, "the job then becomes one of understanding and deepening and sharpening what is already written,"[21] or, *enhancing* the message. This is where you review your manuscript looking for opportunities to use plot, character, setting, and style to strengthen the message, finding new ways to reinforce it.

INTEGRATE THE MESSAGE

A story may be compared to a tapestry,[22] where various colors and patterns have been skillfully woven into a masterpiece, a fine work of art. A tapestry is made by weaving threads, some horizontal and some vertical, over and under each other. The message of a story is like a pattern of thread strands woven into a tapestry: sometimes it's visible and sometimes it's out of sight —but always contributing to the overall effect.[23]

Whether you deliberately planned the story's message from the start, discovered it during the drafting process, or didn't recognize it until you were in the editing and revision phase, one of your tasks is to appropriately integrate message into the story. You need to identify the elemental themes of your story (those of character, plot, setting, and style) and then weave them into your draft in a manner that contributes to a seamless product that achieves the thematic objectives for the project.

RETROFIT THE MESSAGE

What do you do if you don't discover your story's message until after you think your work is complete? This may happen more often than you might think. According to Nancy Kress, "Some writers find that they don't know their themes until they've finished the first draft ... then rewrite with an eye toward balancing."[24] As observed by Peter Selgin, "Until we're done we never have the *whole* picture."[25]

What do you do if you realize that (1) the message you originally planned doesn't fit the story you wrote, (2) a different message from the one you planned has emerged from the story you have written, or (3) the story you've written seems to lack a message?

The choices available to you are: (1) go back and rewrite the story to fit the message you originally planned, (2) adopt the message that has emerged organically from the story, or (3) re-examine your manuscript, looking for the message that ties it all together.

Eight strategies, as outlined in this chapter, provide ample opportunities for authors to develop a story's message.

TAKEAWAYS

- One strategy is to IGNORE message development, just letting the story speak for itself.
- You may PLAN a story's message from the beginning of the project.
- During the process of drafting a manuscript, you may DISCOVER the message.
- EXPLORE the manuscript to find alternative messages.
- From the alternatives available, CHOOSE the most appropriate message.
- Once a message is selected, ENHANCE it to its full potential.
- INTEGRATE the message of your work into a seamless story.
- If necessary, RETROFIT the message into your otherwise complete manuscript.

The next chapter explores how to express theme.

11

EXPRESSING THEME

Between the Lines by Jessica Page Morrell states, "There is no single, proper way to express or state your theme."[1] Earlier in this book, I defined *theme* as what a work of written fiction is about. Such a broad definition reflects my observation that theme means different things to different people, and its meaning depends on the purpose for which it is being communicated. Not surprisingly then, theme may be expressed in a variety of formats.

WORDS OR PHRASES

In an earlier chapter, we looked at the fundamental elements of fiction, their components, and related themes. Many of those themes may be expressed as a word or a short phrase. Themes of plot, such as those expressed by the master plots identified by Ronald B. Tobias, may be expressed as a single word or phrase, such as adventure, revenge, maturation, or forbidden love.[2] A single word or phrase may express a theme that coincides with a *component* of plot structure, such as inciting incident, goal, attempt, obstacle, planning, decision, and resolution. For example, *inciting-incident* themes may include disaster, the arrival of a visitor from afar, or the death of a loved one. Likewise, the plot component of *opposition* could include themes such as discrimination, racism, extremism, cruelty, oppression, or obsession.

Each archetypical character identified by Victoria Lynn Schmidt may be expressed as the word or phrase for that character type: from Seductive Muse/Femme Fatale to the King/Dictator.[3] Various aspects of characterization, such as personal or moral weakness, may offer additional themes, such as lack of self-confidence, prejudice, or greed.

Setting themes may be expressed as words or phrases, for example, Russia, the Great Depression, a North Carolina coastal swamp, inside a computer game, or a post-apocalyptic world. Style themes may include epistolary, multiple-first-person narration, fictitious survival guide, postmodern, stream of consciousness, unreliable narrator, and experimental.

Sometimes all you need to express a theme is a single word or phrase.

SENTENCES

We have already seen that themes of message include allegory, in which the actions and words of the symbols of a story provide insight into the nature of mankind. To adequately express a message, we need a sentence. A story's message may be expressed in sentences with various formats: (1) "what if ..." question, (2) premise, (3) Aristotelean theme, (4) cause-and-effect (if-then) question, (5) imperative sentence, and (6) aphorism.

"What If ..." Question

I suspect that many stories begin with some variation of the "what if ..." question. My first three novels began with the following.

- What if a tornado struck a Boy Scout campsite?
- What if an earthquake struck while you were exploring a cave in the Ozarks?
- What if the War of 1812 was told as a novel?

I view a "what if ..." question as a theme from which a story may grow.

Premise

The word *premise* means "to set forth beforehand,"[4] which implies that authors determine their premise first and then write the story. In reality, fiction writing isn't usually so tidy, and the author may not recognize the premise of a story until later in the process, maybe not until after the first draft is complete.

As described by John Truby, in *The Anatomy of Story*, "The premise is your story stated in one sentence. It is the simplest combination of character and plot and typically consists of some event that starts the action, some sense of the main character, and some sense of the outcome of the story."[5]

Truby writes from the perspective of screenplays and provides some blockbuster examples.

- *The Godfather*: The youngest son of a Mafia family takes revenge on the men who shot his father and becomes the new Godfather.
- *Moonstruck*: While her fiancé visits his mother in Italy, a woman falls in love with the man's brother.
- *Casablanca*: A tough American expatriate rediscovers an old flame only to give her up so that he can fight the Nazis.
- *A Streetcar Named Desire*: An aging beauty tries to get a man to marry her while under constant attack from her sister's brutish husband.
- *Star Wars*: When a princess falls into mortal danger, a young man uses his skills as a fighter to save her and defeat the evil forces of a galactic empire.[6]

I view the *premise* of a work of fiction as a theme by which the story is summarized in one sentence.

Aristotelian Theme

Earlier in this book I described four types of themes that trace their roots back to the ancient Greeks: (1) optimistic, (2) pessimistic, (3) optimistic with an ironic twist, and (4) pessimistic with an ironic twist, which I call *Aristotelian themes.*

Ancient Greeks tended to view their fate as determined by deities who controlled the lives of humans, so Aristotelian themes of the old Greek plays could be expressed as follows.

- You will succeed if the gods support your efforts.
- You will fail if the gods thwart your efforts.
- Even if you succeed, the gods may deny you the full benefit of your efforts.
- Even if you fail, the gods may grant you a benefit.

Today, rather than relying upon the gods to determine our fate, we prefer to take more responsibility for our destiny and expect our fictional characters to do the same, so Aristotelian themes today may be expressed along the following lines.

- If you are persistent in achieving your goal, you will succeed.
- Even if you are persistent in achieving your goal, you will fail.
- Even if you succeed in achieving your goal, you may not receive full benefit for your efforts.
- Even if you fail to achieve your goal, you may benefit somehow.

I believe that any work of fiction that rises to the level of a story may be classified as one of these four types. Aristotelian themes provide a useful foundation for understanding a theme and categorizing it, but to achieve deeper insight, we need more information.

Cause-And-Effect (If-Then) Statement

The message of a story may be expressed as a cause-and-effect statement: For example, the message of the nursery rhyme "Jack and Jill" may be expressed as follows.

- *Personal message*, which relates to the characters in the tale: "Because Jack was careless or unlucky, he failed to achieve his objective."
- *If you ... then you ... message*,[7] which may be expressed in second person: "If you are careless or unlucky, you may fail to achieve your objective."
- *Allegoric message*, which is the story theme expressed as a generalization about the nature of mankind: "Carelessness or bad luck may lead to failure."

Imperative Sentence

A message may be expressed as an instruction or a call to action, in the form of an *imperative sentence*. For example:

- Stand by your friends.
- Do the right thing.
- To thy own self be true.[8]

Aphorism

A message may also be expressed as a *declarative sentence*, a simple statement. Such a statement is sometimes called an *aphorism*, a "terse and often ingenious formulation of a truth or sentiment, usually in a single sentence."[9] Terms similar to *aphorism* include *maxim, adage, bromide, saw,* and *proverb.* For example, "Good things come in small packages," and "Nothing ventured, nothing gained."

Such statements represent a nugget of wisdom or apparent wisdom, and they sound convincing at least until paired with a contrary aphorism.[10] Examples of such dueling aphorisms include the following.

- All good things come to those who wait. / Time and tide wait for no man.
- Birds of a feather flock together. / Opposites attract.
- Actions speak louder than words. / The pen is mightier than the sword.

The message of a story, even an entire genre, may be expressed as an aphorism:

- Love conquers all. (Romance)
- Justice prevails. (Crime)
- Persistence is rewarded. (Any story with a happy, or optimistic, ending)

The word *aphorism* has a positive connotation. Closely related, but with a negative connotation, is *platitude*: "A thought or remark that is flat, dull, trite, or weak."[11]

Authors have a multitude of choices for expressing theme in a sentence.

PARAGRAPHS

The examples above express the theme of a story with a single plot, but the same techniques may also be used to express the theme for each plot in a multiple-plot story. A common structure is for a story to have two plots: one in which the focal character has both an external goal and an internal goal. Often the internal plot reflects a personal or moral weakness that the character needs to address before he or she can achieve the external goal.

For example, in my debut novel, *The Brute*, a sixteen-year-old boy has a clear external goal: to summon help for his injured father and the younger Boy Scouts in his troop. Threatening his ability to achieve his external goal is the challenge he faces in controlling his own violent temper, an internal goal.

Stories with two plots also have two sets of messages. In *The Brute*, (Spoiler alert) the messages for the external plot could be:

- Personal Message: Because Fortney Curtis persisted in his efforts, he was successful in obtaining help for his father and the younger scouts.

- If-then Message: If you persist in your efforts, then you may succeed.
- Allegoric Message: Persistence leads to success.

The messages for the internal plot of *The Brute* could be expressed as follows.

- Personal Message: Because Fortney Curtis learned to control his violent temper, he was also successful in obtaining help for his father and the younger scouts.
- If-then Message: If you can overcome your personal weaknesses, then you may have a greater chance for success with other goals.
- Allegoric Message: Achieving external goals may first require overcoming a personal weakness.

PASSAGE OF WRITING

A work of fiction may have many plots, and each generates its own message, so expressing the themes of a work of fiction might require a *passage of writing*, which I define as two or more consecutive paragraphs with a common purpose. While writing the manuscript for this book, I read bestsellers, and many of those novels featured multiple plots, each of which added depth to the story's overall message, possibly requiring more than one paragraph to express.

COMBINED THEME STATEMENT

Even the simplest stories may have multiple themes, and complex stories may have dozens. One overarching theme may dominate the story, or, alternatively, the meaning of the story may only be represented by multiple themes. The more complex a story, the less likely its messages may be summarized in a short statement.

Themes may be expressed in a variety of formats, which allow plenty of flexibility to do justice to a story's messages.

TAKEAWAYS

- Many themes, including those representing master plots, plot components, archetype characters, settings, and styles, may be expressed as a word or short phrase.
- A story's message may be expressed as a sentence, including a "what-if question, a premise, an Aristotelean theme, a cause-and-effect (if-then) question, an imperative sentence, or an aphorism.
- Expressing the themes of a multiple-plot story may require a paragraph.
- A multi-paragraph passage may be needed to adequately express the themes of a complex story.

The next chapter analyzes the themes of a complex bestselling novel.

12

ANALYSIS OF A BESTSELLER

Spoiler alert. In this chapter we'll look at Jodi Picoult's *Wish You Were Here*, a novel that had a long run on the *USA Today* bestseller list. This story grabbed my attention from the start and continues to resonate with me. The author's website describes the book as "a deeply moving novel about the resilience of the human spirit in a moment of crisis,"[1] which is a nicely crafted expression of theme (and no doubt effective marketing copy), but from the perspective of a writer, teacher, or student of fiction, does it reveal what makes this story special? Let's use the concepts already addressed in this book to analyze the themes of *Wish You Were Here*.

As described earlier, fiction as a form of art can be viewed from the perspective of the heart, the mind, and the craft, each of which may exhibit various qualitative effects and related themes of effect.

QUALITIES OF THE HEART

How was this story EMOTIVE?

- *Wish You Were Here* is an engaging and entertaining story that stimulates a variety of emotions, a roller coaster of emotional experience, for example:
  - The adoration of a young girl for her father
  - Yearning for a mother who chose to be elsewhere
  - The excitement of a challenging career, mixed with the thrill of success and the fear of failure
  - And on and on throughout the story

QUALITIES OF THE MIND

How was *Wish You Were Here* AFFIRMATIVE?

- Message: You may attain career success, even though it may not be in your current job.
- Message: You may find lasting love, although it may not be in your current relationship.
- Message: Kindness and understanding may lead you to accept the sexual orientation of others.

What, if any, aspects of this story were INFORMATIVE?

- Information: Insight into the commercial side of the art world[2]

- Information: Details about the geography and culture of Isabella Island in the Galapagos[3]
- Information: A view from inside the Covid ward of a hospital[4]

How was this story INSTRUCTIVE?

- A glimpse at how a work of art is restored[5]

How was this story ELUCIDATIVE?

- Insight: Supported by reports of people who have had a near-death experience, the possibility that time may be multidimensional.[6]

How was this story INSPIRATIONAL?

- To the extent Jodi Picoult is correct that this story is about "the resilience of the human spirit in a moment of crisis,"[7] it may inspire some of us to greater fortitude.

How was this story MOTIVATIONAL?

- Action: Reading *Wish You Were Here* helped motivate me to google *near-death experience time dimension*, where I learned more about hyperdimensional perspective.

QUALITIES OF CRAFT

- Straightforward, unobtrusive style that doesn't distract the reader from immersing into the tale
- Transitioning into the Galapagos setting without first showing that Diana contracted Covid-19

Next, let's look at the elemental themes, starting with CHARACTER. The story begins with six-year-old Diana recalling when she "helped" her father restore an important work of art. Diana thinks of her mother, a world-renowned photographer, who, as usual, is not home. The story quickly transitions to Friday, March 13, 2020, when Diana, age twenty-nine, works as an art specialist at Sotheby's, the auction company. Diana's current task is to convince a murdered rock star's wife, Kitomi Ito, to consign a famous painting for auction. Diana's boss is Eva, and her best friend is Rodney, who also works at Sotheby's. Diana lives with her longtime boyfriend, Finn, a surgical resident at a local hospital. Later, Diana meets Gabriel, a native of the Galapagos Islands, his daughter (Beatriz), and his mother (Abuela). All these characters, including Diana, are appropriately developed, but each is an "everyman" character, with none rising to a stature that warrants classifying this novel as having a character theme.

The SETTING (place and time) of this story includes three topics worthy of being recognized as fundamental themes: (1) the Covid-19 pandemic, (2) the Galapagos Islands during the lockdown, and (3) the possibility of multidimensional time.

The STYLE of this novel is first-person present tense, written in a straightforward fashion, not drawing attention to itself, or warranting classification as a fundamental theme. The story is presented linearly in time except for Jodi Picoult's choice of how to handle Diana's contraction of the virus and her subsequent comatose days in a hospital. Instead of presenting this part in chronological order, the author pushes the boundary of reliable narration by transitioning directly to the Galapagos, where Diana lives under lockdown for several months before transitioning back to New York, where she wakes up after five days in a coma. The effect of this technique of presentation is that it (1) confuses both character and reader into questioning what is real and what was dream, (2) creates disappointment that the intriguing story unfolding in the Galapagos may have never happened, and (3) places Diana back in a life she now suspects isn't right for her. This stylistic choice adds a dramatic twist that turns what would otherwise have been a good story into a great story.

Wish You Were Here includes multiple external plots and subplots, which are expressed as follows in terms of Diana's goals.

Plots

- For career success as an art expert at Sotheby's
- To marry Finn
- To survive the Covid-19 pandemic, the arrival of which forms the inciting incident of the novel

Subplots

- To return to New York City, or to at least be able to communicate with Finn
- To "be there" for her mother, now in a memory-care home
- To help Beatriz deal with being gay
- To help Gabriel accept the fact that his daughter is homosexual
- To learn the truth about her vivid memories of Galapagos, a mystery
- To become an art therapist

This story also includes multiple internal subplots, expressed here as Diana's plot question regarding that subplot.

Subplots

- Whether selling art is the right career for her
- Whether Finn is the right man for her
- Whether she is falling in love with Gabriel
- How much love, loyalty, and care she owes a mother who wasn't home for much of Diana's childhood
- How she could live simultaneously in two places and timespans

Each plot and subplot generates a message. In *Wish You Were Here*, the pandemic is a plot that runs the length of the novel, and its significance to the story is greater than the other plots, so, by my definition, survival of the pandemic is the MAIN

PLOT, and since Diana survives the pandemic, this plot qualifies as OPTIMISTIC. Diana forgoes her career and leaves Flynn at the end of the novel, so both plots qualify as PESSIMISTIC, but since the character receives a consolation benefit in the ending, or at least the possibility of happiness, each of these two plots qualifies as PESSIMISTIC WITH AN IRONIC TWIST.

The main plot, the survival side of this story, was satisfying, but that isn't what caused the tale to resonate with me. The most important aspects of this novel are (1) a setting in which time and space may be multidimensional and (2) a subplot mystery to determine whether that is possible. That time and space may be hyperdimensional is not a new concept to those of us who have enjoyed sci-fi most of our lives, but the ending of this story "proves" the concept when Dianna "returns" to the Galapagos and is approached from behind by a man who could be the Gabriel of her comatose dream.

Next, let's look at how the theme portfolio of this story may be expressed. By my definition, *Wish You Were Here* has a COMPLEX, COMPOUND STORY (includes two or more plots that run the whole length of the work of fiction *and* at least one subplot). As was addressed in an earlier chapter, expressing the themes of a story with a complicated plot may require more than one sentence. I express this novel's messages in a three-paragraph passage.

> *Wish You Were Here* by Jodi Picoult provides an entertaining roller coaster of emotional experiences, together with themes and messages that affirm cherished beliefs, and provide some informative and instructional content.

The messages of the plots in *Wish You Were Here* are that (1) even though you hope for a long-term romantic relationship, including marriage, with a particular person, you may find true happiness with another, (2) even though your goals include success in a particular career, you may find more satisfaction in another occupation, and (3) with heroic medical care and a little luck, you may be able to survive a deadly pandemic.

Emerging from the setting, the most overriding message of this story is that time may be hyperdimensional, and under certain circumstances, such as a near-death experience, slipping from one time and place to another may be possible. The source of the resonance of this story is the dissonance arising from the possibility of multidimensional time, together with the disturbing stylistic choice of presenting a significant portion of the tale as a comatose dream, which is not revealed as such until later in the novel.

A one-sentence description of theme for a complicated story may be useful for the purposes of marketing, but to gain a better understanding of how fiction works may require more extensive analysis and expression.

TAKEAWAYS

- The concepts presented in this book may be used to analyze a story and then to express its themes.

The next chapter presents a template for analyzing any story.

13

THEME-ANALYSIS TEMPLATE

The purpose of a *theme-analysis template* is to help identify the themes of a work of fiction. As shown earlier in this book, I believe themes may be classified into three groups: (1) qualitative-effect themes, (2) fundamental themes, and (3) message themes. The simplest of tales may have only a few themes, but complicated stories can have layer upon layer of messages, which may be most efficiently identified using a template that can be expanded as needed.

I use the following template to analyze the themes of a story. Not all the sections apply to every story, while more complex tales may require expansion of some sections. For usage flexibility, I maintain the template on a digital document file that may be easily modified as needed.

THEME-ANALYSIS TEMPLATE

Title:_____

By: _____

QUALITATIVE-EFFECT THEMES

Fiction as a form of art can be viewed from the perspective of the heart, the mind, and the craft, each of which may exhibit various qualitative effects. Identify and describe the qualitative-effect themes of this story.

Qualities Of The Heart

How was this story EMOTIVE? Provide examples of emotions stimulated.

_____

Qualities Of The Mind

How was this story AFFIRMATIVE? What messages were reinforced by the story?

_____

What aspects of this story were INFORMATIVE? What knowledge was provided by the story?

_____

How was this story INSTRUCTIVE? What activities did the story show you how to do?

_____

How was this story ELUCIDATIVE? What insight was provided by the story?

_____

How was this story INSPIRATIONAL? In what ways did this story fill you with an urge to do or feel something?

_____

How was this story MOTIVATIONAL? In what ways did this story propel you toward action?

_____

Qualities Of Craft

Note and categorize the writing techniques used by the author.

_____

FUNDAMENTAL THEMES

Identify and describe the fundamental themes of this story.

Character Themes

List the most important characters in this story, along with their classification as protagonist, antagonist, ally, love interest, etc. Note if any of the characters qualify as an archetype or if "everyman" best describes them. Identify which, if any, of the above so dominates the story that he or she could be described as a theme; i.e., qualifying the work as a "character story." Describe what makes this character so noteworthy.

Setting Themes

TIME: Describe the role played by time in this story (for example, antagonist, ally, etc.). Note the author's style of presenting and accounting for time. State the timespan of this story. Note any other aspects of time that were unique or otherwise stood out.

LOCATION: Describe the role played by location in this story (for example, antagonist, ally, etc.). Could the location(s) have been changed without meaningfully changing the story? If not, why not? Note any other aspects of the location that were unique or otherwise stood out.

MILIEU: Describe the greater social, political, and economic environment of this story. Identify and describe any groups of people in the story. Note any other aspects of the time and place that were unique or otherwise stood out.

Style Themes

Describe the style with which this story was presented. Incorporate your notes under the Qualities of Craft section of this template. Note any stylistic variations that stood out.

Theme Themes

Describe any messages included in the story. Note any promotional messages.

Plot Themes

State as a goal of the character any **external plots** of this story (external plots that run more or less the entire length of the story).

State as a goal of the character any **external subplots** of this story (external plots that run less than the entire length of the story).

From the character's point of view, form a question that defines any **internal plots** (internal plots that run more or less the entire length of the story).

From the character's point of view, form a question that defines any **internal subplots** (internal plots that run less than the entire length of the story).

Identify the **main plot** of this story.

Message Themes

For each plot listed above, identify its Aristotelean category: (1) find the protagonist's goal at the beginning, (2) note whether and how that goal is achieved at the end, and (3) classify the plot as optimistic, pessimistic, or ironic. If ironic, classify the story as optimistic or pessimistic with an ironic twist.

THEMATIC EXPRESSION

From the messages noted above, develop a thematic expression of appropriate form and length for the story.

TAKEAWAYS

- A theme-analysis template is a useful tool for identifying and categorizing the themes of a story.

The next two chapters utilize the theme-analysis template to study (1) a very simple story: "Little Miss Muffet" by Mother Goose and (2) the more complicated tale of *Where the Crawdads Sing* by Delia Owens.

THEME-ANALYSIS TEMPLATE— SIMPLE STORY

To illustrate how a theme-analysis template may be used for a very simple story, let's look at the nursery rhyme of "Little Miss Muffet" by Mother Goose, which is included below.

> *Little Miss Muffet*
> *Sat on a tuffet,*
> *Eating her curds and whey;*
> *Along came a spider,*
> *Who sat down beside her,*
> *And frightened Miss Muffet away.*[1]

The Theme-Analysis Temple is designed to be used with any work of fiction, from the simplest to the most complex. Since "Little Miss Muffet" is a very simple story, I wouldn't expect every line of the template to apply. Rather than duplicate the entire form here (with a bunch of "No" or "Not Applicable" answers), I'll just include the most relevant issues, with my responses in bold type.

THEME-ANALYSIS TEMPLATE
Title: "Little Miss Muffet"
By: Mother Goose

QUALITATIVE-EFFECT THEMES

Fiction as a form of art can be viewed from the perspective of the heart, the mind, and the craft, each of which may exhibit various qualitative effects. Identify and describe the qualitative-effect themes of this story.

Qualities Of The Heart

How was this story EMOTIVE? Provide examples of emotions stimulated.

- **This story is entertaining in that it is told in rhyme and that it provokes dramatic imagery evoking the emotions of (1) fear (A spider sat down beside her!), (2) relief that the spider didn't bite her, and (3) humor from a near-miss experience.**

FUNDAMENTAL THEMES

Identify and describe the fundamental themes of this story.

Character Themes

List the most important characters in this story, along with their classification as protagonist, antagonist, ally, love interest, etc. Note if any of the characters qualify as an archetype or if "everyman" best describes them. Identify which, if any, of the above so dominates the story that he or she could be described as a theme, i.e., qualifying the work as a "character story." Describe what makes this character so noteworthy.

- **Miss Muffet (protagonist)**
- **Spider (antagonist)**
- **Neither of these characters is developed enough to qualify as an archetype, nor would the story qualify as a "character story."**

Setting Themes

TIME: Describe the role played by time in this story (for example, antagonist, ally, etc.). Note the author's style of presenting and accounting for time in this story. State the timespan of this story. Describe the milieu of the story. Note any other aspects of time that were unique or otherwise stood out.

- **This is a very short story (a nursery rhyme), and time plays no significant role.**
- **The time span of this story could be as short as a few seconds.**

LOCATION: Describe the role played by location in this story (for example, antagonist, ally, etc.). Could the location(s) in this story have been changed without meaningfully changing the story? If not, why not? Note any other aspects of the location that were unique or otherwise stood out.

- **The location of the story is a *tuffet* (a low stool, or footstool), but that detail could be changed in any number of ways without meaningfully altering the story.**

Style Themes

Describe the style with which this story was presented. Incorporate your notes under the Qualities of Craft section of this template. Note any stylistic variations that stood out.

- **This story is presented in the stylistic form of a poem, more specifically a nursery rhyme.**

Plot Themes

Identify and list the plots in this story.

State as a goal of the character any **external plots** of this story (external plots that run more or less the entire length of the story).

- **Goal: to eat curds and whey.**

Message Themes

For each plot listed above, identify its **Aristotelean category**: (1) find the protagonist's goal at the beginning of the story, (2) note whether and how that goal is achieved at the end of the story, and (3) classify the plot as optimistic, pessimistic, or ironic. If ironic, classify the story as optimistic or pessimistic with an ironic twist.

- **This story has only one plot.**
- **Miss Muffet's goal is to eat curds and whey.**
- **The obstacle that complicates achieving her goal is a spider.**
- **The ending shows Miss Muffet running away.**
- **Since Miss Muffet failed to achieve her goal, this is a pessimistic plot, and since it didn't have an ironic twist at the end, it doesn't qualify as ironic.**

For each plot listed above, **express** its message.

- **Personal message: Because Miss Muffet lacked courage, she failed to eat her meal.**
- **If ... then ... message: If you let fear overtake your emotions, you may fail to achieve your goal.**
- **Aristotelean message: "Lack of courage in the face of danger may lead to failure."**

THEMATIC EXPRESSION

From the messages noted above, develop a thematic expression of appropriate form and length for the story.

- **This simple little story has entertained children for centuries, generating resonance by stimulating (1) the emotion of fear (Eek! A spider sat down beside her.), (2) relief that she escaped danger (hear nervous giggles), and (3) pleasure (see smiles) from its style of presentation as a rhyme.**

TAKEAWAYS

- The theme-analysis template provides a useful tool for evaluating even the simplest of stories.

The next chapter analyzes a much more complicated story.

15

THEME-ANALYSIS TEMPLATE—COMPLEX STORY

Spoiler alert. In this chapter, we'll look in-depth at *Where the Crawdads Sing* by Delia Owens. This story perplexed me, challenging me to understand why I kept thinking about it and how that effect was accomplished. In the theme-analysis template below, my responses are shown in bold print.

THEME-ANALYSIS TEMPLATE
Title: *Where the Crawdads Sing*
By: **Delia Owens**

QUALITATIVE-EFFECT THEMES

Fiction as a form of art can be viewed from the perspective of the heart, the mind, and the craft, each of which may exhibit various qualitative effects. Identify and describe the qualitative-effect themes of this story.

Qualities Of The Heart

How was this story EMOTIVE? Provide examples of emotions stimulated.

This is an engaging and entertaining story that stimulates a variety of emotions, a roller coaster of emotional experience, for example:

- **Alarm and sadness when Kya's mother abandons her**
- **Shame and humiliation when schoolgirls laugh at Kya**
- **Joy as Kya feeds the seagulls**
- **And on and on throughout the story**

Qualities Of The Mind

How was this story AFFIRMATIVE? What messages were reinforced by the story?

- **Message: Persistence pays.**
- **Message: If you can't count on others, you must rely on yourself.**
- **Message: A humble background does not limit personal success.**

What aspects of this story were INFORMATIVE? What knowledge was provided by the story?

- **Information: The differences between a marsh and a swamp**
- **Information: Details of marsh wildlife**
- **Information: Details about the mating habits of marsh creatures**

How was this story INSTRUCTIVE? What activities did the story show you how to do?

- **Information: Survival skills in a coastal marsh**
- **A glimpse at how to harvest mussels and dry fish**
- **How to develop an illustrated nature book**

How was this story ELUCIDATIVE? What insight was provided by the story?

- **Insight into the culture of a coastal marsh community**

How was this story INSPIRATIONAL? In what ways did this story fill you with an urge to do or feel something?

I suspect that many female readers (and quite a few guys, including me) found this story inspirational:

- **Despite substantial disadvantages, Kya grew into a responsible and successful adult.**
- **Even in times of great hardship, she found a way to take heart and persist.**
- **An optimistic underdog story is inherently inspirational.**

How was this story MOTIVATIONAL? In what ways did this story propel you toward action?

- **This story caused me to self-evaluate and then to resolve to improve and do more with my life.**

Qualities Of Craft

Note and categorize the writing techniques used by the author.

- **The narration is in the third-person singular.**

- The tone of the narration is straightforward.
- The story includes passages of narrative description and narrative exposition, some with lyrical language.
- Most of the story is presented from the protagonist's point of view.
- Some chapters are written from the point of view of other characters.
- Starting with the prologue, the murder mystery is told in occasional chapters interspersed between chapters representing the rest of the timeline.

FUNDAMENTAL THEMES

Identify and describe the fundamental themes of this story.

Character Themes

List the most important characters in this story, along with their classification as protagonist, antagonist, ally, love interest, etc. Note if any of the characters qualify as an archetype or if "everyman" best describes them. Identify which, if any, of the above so dominates the story that he or she could be described as a theme, i.e., qualifying the work as a "character story." Describe what makes this character so noteworthy.

- **The story opens with a six-year-old girl named Kya, who has many antagonists throughout the story: her family members, who desert her; the local town folk; a truant officer; a sexual predator; the sheriff; and a prosecutor.**

- Kya has a few allies: Jump'n, the dockside store owner, and his wife, Mabel; her friend Tate; and eventually, a publisher and a defense attorney.
- Tate Walker and Chase Andrews develop into love interests.
- After betraying Kya, Chase becomes a sexual predator.
- One of the most dominant and interesting characters is the marsh itself, which acts as Kya's teacher and her protector.
- Kya's most noteworthy characteristic is her dogged resilience.
- All of Kya's adversaries are either bigger, older, more worldly, or more powerful than her, which makes Kya a posterchild for an archetype character, the underdog.
- By far, the dominant character in this novel is Kya herself, so much so that the character theme (or the title) of this novel could be "Kya, the Marsh Girl."

Setting Themes

TIME: Describe the role played by time in this story (for example, antagonist, ally, etc.). Note the author's style of presenting and accounting for time in this story. State the timespan of this story. Note any other aspects of time that were unique or otherwise stood out.

- Starting with the prologue and continuing until the ending, the story is told in a nonlinear fashion, with

the murder mystery presented parallel to the rest of the tale. The chapter headings partially mitigate this disjointed presentation by stating the month and year.
- **Timespan: 1952-1970**
- **Although the timeframe of the story qualifies it as historical fiction, and that adds an interesting dimension to the story, this tale could have been told in other timeframes and, with a few adjustments, could have been equally interesting. Categorizing this tale as historical fiction may be technically correct, but that wouldn't help much in the quest to understand why this novel resonates.**

LOCATION: Describe the role played by location in this story (for example, antagonist, ally, etc.). Could the location(s) have been changed without meaningfully changing the story? If not, why not? Note any other aspects of the location that were unique or otherwise stood out.

- The marsh is not just a setting; it's another character. In addition to becoming Kya's teacher and protector, the marsh supplies her with friends (the gulls).
- By the novel's end, Kya returns the favor by becoming the protector of the marsh, defending it against commercial development.
- The marsh permeates this story so much that the story could be described as a celebration of nature.
- Studying and painting the plants and animals of the marsh became Kya's life's work.

- The setting for this novel is a North Carolina coastal-marsh community, which is integral to this tale. The choice of a different type of setting would require significant changes to the story.

MILIEU: Describe the greater social, political, and economic environment of this story. Identify and describe any groups of people. Note any other aspects of the time and place that were unique or otherwise stood out.

- Much of the antagonism Kya receives is dished out from the small town near the marsh, particularly the white community. So much so that the town takes on the role of an adversary, a collective villain.
- The setting theme for this story is a vibrant coastal marsh acting as the main character's ally while much of the local white community takes on the role of an adversary.

Style Themes

Describe the style with which this story was presented. Incorporate your notes under the Qualities of Craft section of this template. Note any stylistic variations that stand out.

- Regarding style, this novel is written mostly in straightforward, third-person singular narration.
- Most of the tale is written from the perspective of the protagonist, although some chapters are written from the point of view of other characters.

- Some passages of narrative description or exposition include lyrical language, which complements the setting.
- Starting with the prologue, the murder mystery is told in occasional chapters interspersed between chapters representing the rest of the timeline, adding to the dramatic effect of the story, but it also interrupts the story's flow. This disjointed presentation is mitigated by including the story year in each chapter heading.

Theme Themes

Describe any messages included in the story. Note any promotional messages.

- The overriding message of this story coincides with the master plot of the underdog, in this case a young female.
- A subplot promotional message in this story is that the coastal marsh is an environmental jewel worthy of being cherished and protected.

Plot Themes

- In my initial analysis of the story, I found no plot that ran the entire length of the novel.
- Of the many plots in this story, most do not run the length of the novel: (1) The survival and coming-of-age plots end in 1964, when Kya turns eighteen, (2)

the ascendency plot doesn't begin until after Kya is an adult in 1964, and (3) in the real time of the story (from 1952 to 1970), the murder mystery doesn't begin until the body is found in 1969. Each of the plots described above is a *subplot*.
- This perplexed me: How could such an interesting story not have a single plot that runs the entire length of the story? Without a backbone to the story, it should be a mess, but it isn't. Upon further reflection, I noted that I had identified Kya's character as an underdog archetype, and then I recalled that underdog is also a master plot.
- An alternative explanation of the story's structure is that: (1) the murder mystery/courtroom drama plot is the main plot and (2) the rest of the story, which includes over half of the tale, is backstory. I discarded this conclusion because this tale is about much more than a mystery.

State as a goal of the character any **external plots** of this story (external plots that run more or less the entire length of the story).

- **To succeed in achieving her objectives despite overwhelming disadvantage and opposition (an underdog plot).**

State as a goal of the character any **external subplots** of this story (external plots that run less than the entire length of the story).

This story includes multiple external subplots:

- To provide the basic requirements of sustaining herself physically, a survival plot
- To learn more about the marsh environment and the life it contains (which shows that education may be attained by informal means)
- To write, illustrate, and publish nature books and become economically independent
- To protect the marsh from real-estate development
- To find love with Chase (until he marries another woman)
- To protect herself from a sexual predator (Chase)
- To avoid being arrested
- To avoid being convicted of murder

From the character's point of view, form a question that defines any **internal plots** (internal plots that run more or less the entire length of the story).

- From the beginning to the ending, can Kya, as an archetype underdog character, fill the holes in her life: the lack of family, friendship, and love?

From the character's point of view, form a question that defines any **internal subplots** (internal plots that run less than the entire length of the story).

- Can Kya overcome her sense of abandonment, by her mother, her brother, and her father?

- Can Kya overcome the loneliness of her life?
- Can Kya mature into a responsible adult while growing up in the isolation of a marsh?
- Can Kya overcome a broken heart caused by the abandonment of Tate Walker?
- Can Kya overcome the betrayal of Chase Andrews, who professes his love for her but marries another?

Identify the **main plot** of this story.

- The main plot of *Where the Crawdads Sing* is the master plot of the underdog, which features a character whose attempts to achieve goals are thwarted by overwhelming opposition.

Message Themes

For each plot listed above, identify its **Aristotelean category**: (1) find the protagonist's goal at the beginning, (2) note whether and how that goal is achieved at the end, and (3) classify the plot as optimistic, pessimistic, or ironic. If ironic, classify the story as optimistic or pessimistic with an ironic twist.

In each of the following subplots, Kya is successful in achieving her objective, so each generates an optimistic message.

- Kya succeeds in providing the basic requirements to sustain herself physically, so the survival subplot is

an optimistic story, with the message that persistence and ingenuity can lead to success.
- Using the marsh as an ally, Kya successfully evades truant officers and others who seek to "help" her, which creates the message that with acquired skills and the use of available resources, you can succeed.
- Kya finds solace in the poetry of Amanda Hamilton.
- With the marsh as her classroom, art supplies abandoned by her mother, and books provided by her friend Tate, Kya learns about the world around her, showing that, with determination, education may be attained by nontraditional means.
- After Tate suggests that Kya submit her art for consideration, and she is encouraged by a publisher, she becomes financially independent as an author-illustrator, showing that a career may bloom from doing what you love.
- Kya's success in survival, education, and art also shows that Kya has matured into a responsible young adult.
- Kya's financial success enables her to purchase the marsh and place it in a trust to protect it from development.

In each of the following subplots, Kya fails to achieve her objective, so each generates a pessimistic message.

- Kya never learned the fate of her father, who simply disappeared.

- Kya hoped to find love with Tate, who abandoned her after he left for college.
- Kya hoped to find love with Chase, until she learned that he had married another woman.
- Kya's attempts to avoid arrest eventually failed when she was caught boating in open water.

Each of the following subplots ends with an ironic twist.

- Despite Kya's yearning for the return of her mother, she never does, but Kya eventually learns that her mother never forgot her, creating an ironic twist that qualifies this subplot as pessimistic with an ironic twist.
- Kya's brother returned to provide her with moral support, but only after learning that she had been charged with murder.
- Kya eventually found love with Tate, but only after she abandoned hope and found peace with her solitary, self-sufficient life.
- Kya successfully thwarted Chase's sexual attack, but that led to her being a suspect in his death.
- Kya was acquitted of killing Chase, but in the end, we learn that she had committed cold-blooded murder and got away with it.

The main plot is that of an underdog who begins the tale with overwhelming disadvantages and adversity but who, through persistence and creativity, attained remarkable achievement. In an ironic twist at the end, we learn that

Kya's accomplishments also included writing poetry under the pen name of Amanda Hamilton.

Thematic Expression

From the messages noted above, develop a thematic expression of appropriate form and length for the story.

Where the Crawdads Sing by Delia Owens is a novel filled with powerful themes. It's the story of "Kya, the Marsh Girl," who could be a poster child for the archetype character of the underdog. The protagonist's life is portrayed quite appropriately through the master plot of the underdog, as Kya overcomes substantial disadvantages to achieve remarkable success. The title refers to the setting, the portion of a North Carolina coastal marsh "far in the bush where critters are wild, still behaving like critters."[1] The style fragments time, as a subplot is presented in alternating chapters parallel to the timeline of the main story. The ending shows that this is an optimistic tale with an ironic double-twist ending.

Not only is this tale a celebration of nature, but the setting also becomes a character, providing Kya with sustenance and protection when she is abandoned in the marsh at a young age. The community also includes a small town, whose residents largely comprise a collective villain, as they try to "help" Kya, torment her, or just dismiss her as trash. Only in the "colored" part of town does she find loyal allies. Two of the local boys befriend Kya and become romantic interests, but one abandons her when he leaves for college and the other betrays Kya by marrying someone else.

Despite overwhelming disadvantages, Kya manages to survive and eventually thrive in the marsh by herself. She finds companionship with the seagulls and is inspired by poetry. She draws and paints local wildlife and has become a successful nature book author and illustrator. When one of the local boys is found dead, Kya becomes the primary suspect and is eventually captured, jailed, and tried for murder, then acquitted.

The style of this story is straightforward but with some lyrical language. The murder-mystery subplot begins in the prologue for dramatic effect and is continued in segments throughout the novel, giving the mistaken impression that the mystery is the main plot when it doesn't actually start until after Kya is an adult.

Not only is Kya an underdog archetype character, but the underdog master plot is the main plot of the story, in which Kya overcomes disadvantages and opposition to become a responsible adult, eventually safeguarding the marsh from development. Her childhood boyfriend returns from college and earns back her trust and love.

Not until after her death do we learn, in an ironic twist, that Kya was also Amanda Hamilton, in whose poetry Kya found solace throughout the story. And then, to complete an ironic double twist, we learn from one of Kya's poems that she behaved like a cunning critter to protect herself from her former boyfriend, turned sexual predator, by successfully

planning and executing the murder for which she was tried and acquitted. Go girl!

TAKEAWAYS

- The theme-analysis template provides a useful tool for evaluating even the most complex stories.

In this chapter, we analyzed the themes in a bestseller and how they led to resonance. In the next chapter, we'll look at how to troubleshoot a manuscript for theme.

16

TROUBLESHOOTING A MANUSCRIPT FOR THEME

A great time to use the concepts covered in this book is right after you've completed the first draft of a story and are ready to troubleshoot prior to revision. This chapter shows how to analyze a manuscript for theme. To keep this exercise manageable, I've selected a short piece of writing, the public-domain version of *Puss in Boots*,[1] as a proxy for the first draft of a story. Fairy tales tend to be stories that are good enough to stand the test of time, but the craft of writing fiction has come a long way in the two hundred years since many of the European folktales were first printed. I start by reminding myself that any piece of writing, even a classic tale, can be improved, so I shouldn't hesitate to identify potential improvements.

Prior to beginning the process of revision, it's a good idea to establish a goal for the project. In this example, my objective in revising *Puss in Boots* is to stay true to the traditional story while more fully developing it, if not to a full-length novel, at least to the length of a novella.

The public-domain version of *Puss in Boots*, as transcribed from www.grimmstories.com, is included below. I encourage you to do your own read-through of this story, keeping in mind the concepts already addressed in this book. Jot down your observations regarding the story's themes. I'll ask you to refer to your notes later in this chapter.

PUSS IN BOOTS
by the Brothers Grimm
(Public-Domain Version, lightly edited by Mike Klaassen)
Source: www.grimmstories.com/*en/grimm_fairy-tales/puss_in_boots*. June 15, 2021.

A miller had three sons, his mill, a donkey, and a tomcat. The sons had to grind, the donkey had to get grain and carry flour away, and the cat had to catch mice. When the miller died, the three brothers divided their inheritance. The oldest received the mill, the second the donkey, and the third the tomcat.

The third son was sad and said, "I got all the worst. My oldest brother can mill, and my second can ride on his donkey. What can I do with the tomcat? I'll make a pair of fur gloves from his pelt and be done with it."

"Listen," said the tomcat, who had understood everything the third son said, "you do not need to kill me to get a pair of bad gloves from my pelt. Have a pair of boots made for me, so I can go out and be seen among the people, and you will soon benefit."

The miller's son was astonished that the tomcat could speak. Just then a shoemaker walked by, and the son called him in and had a pair of boots made for the tomcat.

The tomcat put the boots on, poured some corn into a sack, and tied it shut with a string. He threw the sack over his back and ran out the door like a human.

In those days the land was reigned by a king who liked to eat partridges so much that none could be obtained. The forest was full of partridges, but they were so shy that no hunter could get them. The tomcat knew of this and resolved to do better.

When the tomcat reached the forest, he opened the sack and spread some corn around it. He laid the string on the grass and led it behind a hedge. There he hid himself and lurked.

Partridges soon came running for the corn and, one after another hopped into the sack. When a good quantity of partridges were in the sack, the tomcat pulled the string closed. He ran to the sack and, one by one, grabbed each bird and wrung its neck until it was dead. He stuffed the partridges back into the sack, tossed it over his shoulder, and went straight away to the king's palace.

The watchman cried, "Halt! Where to?"

"To the king," answered the tomcat.

"Are you crazy? A tomcat to the king?"

Another watchman said, "Just let him go. The king is often bored, and maybe the tomcat can amuse him."

When the tomcat came before the king, the cat bowed and said, "My Herr, the Graf, sends greetings and these partridges, which he just caught in snares."

The king, astonished by the beautiful partridges, knew not how to contain his pleasure. He commanded that the tomcat be given as much gold out of the treasure chamber as he could carry in his sack. "Take the gold to your Herren and thank him many times for his gift."

The miller's son sat at home at his window, supporting his head on his hand and thinking about how he had spent his last money on the tomcat's boots. He wondered what things the cat would bring back to him.

The tomcat stepped into the house, pulled the sack from his back, opened the bag, and poured out the gold in front of the miller. "Now you have something for the boots. The king also greets you and says many thanks to you."

The miller was glad about the wealth, without fully understanding how it came to be. But the tomcat, as he took off his boots, told him everything, then said, "You have money enough now, but you should not be satisfied. Tomorrow I will put my boots on again, and you will become richer still. I told the king that you are a Graf."

The next day, the tomcat went, well-booted, to hunting again and brought the king a rich catch. So, it went on for many days, and the tomcat brought home gold each day and was so popular with the king that he was allowed to come in and go out and prowl around the palace wherever he wanted.

One day, the tomcat stood in the king's kitchen by the stove and warmed himself, when in came the coachman cursing. "I wish the king and the princess were at the executioner! I wanted to go to Wirtshaus to drink and play cards, but now I must drive them to the lake." As the tomcat heard that, he snuck home and told his Herren: "If a Graf you want to be and become rich, come outside with me to the lake and bathe yourself therein."

The miller's son did not know what to say to that, but he followed the tomcat, went with him, undressed, and sprang into the water. The tomcat took his clothes, carried them away, and hid them.

No sooner was he finished with that than the king came driving by. The tomcat immediately began to lament: "Ach! All merciful king! Mein Herr bathed himself here in the lake, thereon a thief came and stole his clothes that lay on the shore. Now the Herr Graf is in the water and cannot come out, and if he stays in any longer, he will catch a cold and die."

When the king heard that, he called a halt and sent one of his people to bring back some of the king's clothes. The Herr Graf put on the magnificent clothes, and because the king thought he had received the partridges from the Graf, the king invited him to sit with them in the carriage. The princess was pleased, because the Graf was young and handsome, and she liked him quite well.

The tomcat suggested that the king follow him to the Graf's palace, and the king eagerly agreed. The tomcat went ahead and came to a large pasture, where over a hundred people were making hay. "Who does this pasture belong to?" said the tomcat.

"The great magician."

"Listen, the king will soon drive by. When he asks who the pasture belongs to, answer Herr Graf. If you don't, you will all be struck dead."

Thereon the tomcat went farther and came to a large grain field. There stood over two hundred people harvesting the grain. "Whose grain is this?"

"The great magician."

"Listen, the king will drive by soon. When he asks who the grain belongs to, answer Herr Graf. If you do not do that, you will all be struck dead."

Finally, the tomcat came to a magnificent forest. There stood more than three hundred people, felling big oak trees and chopping wood. "Whose forest is this?"

"The great magician."

"Listen, the king will drive by soon. When he asks who the forest belongs to, answer Herr Graf. If you do not, you will all be killed."

The tomcat went still farther. The people looked after him, and because he looked much like a human walking in boots, they were afraid of him.

He soon came to the magician's palace, and he stepped boldly in front of him.

The magician looked at him contemptuously and asked him what he wanted.

The tomcat bowed and said, "I have heard that you can transform yourself into any animal that you choose. A hound, a fox, or even a wolf, I might well believe, but not an elephant. That seems impossible, and therefore I have come to convince myself."

The magician said proudly, "That is a trifle to me." And in the blink of an eye, he was transformed into an elephant.

"That is impressive, but how about a lion?"

"That is also nothing," said the magician and stood as a lion in front of the tomcat.

The tomcat made as if startled, and he cried, "That is unbelievable and unheard of. Still more impressive would be transforming yourself into a tiny animal such as a mouse. Then you would certainly be the greatest magician in the world, but that would probably be too difficult for you."

The magician was flattered by the sweet words and said, "Oh, dear cat-let, that I can also do." And he sprang as a mouse around the room.

The tomcat was after him, caught the mouse with one jump, and ate him.

The king was still riding in the coach with the Graf and the princess and came to the large pasture. "Who does this hay belong to?" asked the king.

"The Herr Graf," cried all, as the tomcat commanded them.

"Thou have a pretty piece of land, Herr Graf," said he.

Thereafter they came to the large grain field. "Who does the grain belong to, you people?"

"The Herr Graf."

"Ei! Herr Graf! Big estates!"

Thereon to the forest. "You people, who does this wood belong to?"

"The Herr Graf."

The king was astonished even more and said, "Thou must be a rich man, Herr Graf, I do not believe that I have such a magnificent forest."

Finally, they came to the palace, where the tomcat stood at the top of the stairs. As the wagon stopped below, the tomcat sprang down, opened the door, and said, "Herr King, thou comest to the palace of my Herr, the Graf. This honors him and makes him happy."

The king stepped out and marveled at the magnificent building that was almost as large and beautiful as his own palace. The Graf led the princess up the stairs into a hall that shimmered with gold and precious stones.

Soon the princess was promised to the Graf. When the king died, the Graf became king, and the booted tomcat became the prime minister.

If you haven't done so already, finish your notes regarding the themes of "Puss in Boots."

TROUBLESHOOTING STEPS

In my book *Third-Person Possessed: How to Write Page-Turning Fiction for 21st Century Readers*, I present a series of troubleshooting steps designed to put a story in perspective and to reveal weaknesses that may be addressed. The techniques include a read-through, a premise, a one-paragraph summary, a chapter-by-chapter outline, a scene-and-sequel analysis, a fiction-writing-mode analysis, and a revision to-do list. To that list I add the theme-analysis template, which is used below to study *Puss in Boots* (my responses in bold font).

THEME-ANALYSIS TEMPLATE
Title: **Puss in Boots**
By: **Brothers Grimm**

QUALITATIVE-EFFECT THEMES

Fiction as a form of art can be viewed from the perspective of the heart, the mind, and the craft, each of which may exhibit various qualitative effects. Identify and describe the qualitative-effect themes of this story.

Qualities Of The Heart

How was this story EMOTIVE? Provide examples of emotions stimulated.

This is an engaging and entertaining story that stimulates a variety of emotions, for example:

- Frustration by the miller's third son at inheriting only a tomcat
- Concern by the tomcat upon hearing that the miller's youngest son planned to turn him into a pair of gloves
- The king's delight at receiving partridges for his meal
- And so on

Qualities Of The Mind

How was this story AFFIRMATIVE? What messages were reinforced by the story?

- **Persistence pays.**
- **Even in the face of overwhelming opposition, success may be achieved with creativity.**

What aspects of this story were INFORMATIVE? What knowledge was provided by the story?

- **None**

How was this story INSTRUCTIVE? What activities did the story show you how to do?

- **How to catch partridges with string, corn, and a bag.**

How was this story ELUCIDATIVE? What insight was provided by the story?

- **None**

How was this story INSPIRATIONAL? In what ways did this story fill you with an urge to do or feel something?

- **A humble background doesn't preclude extraordinary success.**

How was this story MOTIVATIONAL? In what ways did this story propel you toward action?

- **None**

Qualities Of Craft

Note and categorize the writing techniques used by the author.

- **Told in third-person omniscient narration as a fairy tale.**

FUNDAMENTAL THEMES

Identify and describe the fundamental themes of this story.

Character Themes

List the most important characters in this story, along with their classification as protagonist, antagonist, ally, love interest, etc. Note if any of the characters qualify as an archetype or if "everyman" best describes them. Identify which, if any, of the above so dominates the story that he or she could be described as a theme; i.e., qualifying the work as a "character story." Describe what makes this character so noteworthy.

- **The cast of characters in this story includes Puss, a miller, his three sons, a king, a princess, and a great magician. Although each of the characters has a role, the character theme of this story, as confirmed by the tale's title, is the protagonist, Puss, a tomcat who speaks, wears boots, and walks upright.**
- **The protagonist of this story is a cat but not just any old cat. This is a tomcat with superpowers: he can walk on his hind legs, he can talk, he can manipulate the people around him, and he can develop complex schemes. The character-theme of this story is a fantasy tomcat named Puss, who so dominates the story that it qualifies as a character story about Puss.**

Setting Themes

TIME: Describe the role played by time in this story (for example, antagonist, ally, etc.). Note the author's style of presenting and accounting for time. State the timespan of this story. Note any other aspects of time that were unique or otherwise stood out.

- **The events of this story are presented in chronological order, without time playing a significant factor.**
- **The timespan of the story is unclear as to how much time passes between the beginning and the ending.**

LOCATION: Describe the role played by location in this story (for example, antagonist, ally, etc.). Could the location(s) have been changed without meaningfully changing the story? If no, why not? Note any other aspects of location that were unique or otherwise stood out.

- **The setting of this story is a fantasy feudal kingdom, which includes magic as a prominent feature.**
- **Although the exact location is unclear, the language of the story includes German titles and other words.**
- **Regardless of the exact location and the language spoken, that the setting is a magical feudal kingdom is essential to the tale. Another setting would radically change the story.**

MILIEU: Describe the greater social, political, and economic environment of this story. Identify and describe any groups of people in the story. Note any other aspects of the time and place that were unique or otherwise stood out.

- **Befitting a fairy tale, the milieu is a magical, fantasy feudal kingdom, which serves as the story's setting theme.**
- **The milieu includes two kingdoms: one ruled by a benevolent king and the other by a great magician.**

Style Themes

Describe the style with which this story was presented. Incorporate your notes under the Qualities of Craft section of this template. Note any stylistic variations that stood out.

- ***Puss in Boots* is presented in the distant, delayed, third-person narration often found in literature, including fairy tales. I categorize the style-theme of the story as classic omniscience.**

Theme Themes

Describe any messages included in the story. Note any promotional messages.

- **In my read-through of this story, I didn't detect the promotion of any concept, moral, or philosophy.**

- I cringe at reading a story in which wealth and position are accomplished through dishonesty and trickery.
- The message of the public-domain version of *Puss in Boots* is that deceit may be rewarded with wealth and power.

Plot Themes

State as a goal of the character any **external plots** of this story (external plots that run more or less the entire length of the story).

- The inciting incident of the public-domain version of *Puss in Boots* is the death of the miller.
- Shortly thereafter, the tomcat says, "You do not need to kill me, to get a pair of bad gloves from my pelt. Let a pair of boots be made for me, so that I can go out and be seen among the people, and then you will soon benefit."
- The phrase *then you will soon benefit* establishes the tomcat's story goal: to help the miller's youngest son.
- The tomcat then performs a series of activities that increase the miller's son's wealth and status.
- This plot neatly fits the pattern of the ascension master plot, which, by my analysis, establishes ascension as a plot theme of this story.

State as a goal of the character any **external subplots** of this story (external plots that run less than the entire length of the story).

- **I identified no external subplots in this story.**

From the character's point of view, form a question that defines any **internal plots** (internal plots that run more or less the entire length of the story).

- **I identified no internal plots in this story.**

From the character's point of view, form a question that defines any **internal subplots** (internal plots that run less than the entire length of the story).

- **I identified no internal subplots in this story.**

Identify the **main plot** of this story.

- **The *only* plot in this story is, by default, the main plot.**

Message Themes

For each plot listed above, identify its Aristotelean category: (1) find the protagonist's goal at the beginning of the story, (2) note whether and how that goal is achieved at the end of the story, and (3) classify the plot as optimistic, pessimistic, or ironic. If ironic, classify the story as optimistic or pessimistic with an ironic twist.

- **The happy ending of this tale qualifies it as an *optimistic story*, a tale in which the story's goal is achieved.**
- **Although Puss achieves his goal using cleverness, the ending does not include an ironic twist.**

Thematic Expression

From the messages noted above, develop a thematic expression of appropriate form and length for the story.

- **The message of this story is that deceit and trickery may help you achieve great success.**

Earlier in this chapter I asked you to read through the public-domain version of *Puss in Boots* and to jot down notes regarding the story's themes, keeping in mind the concepts already covered in this book. Now I want you to consult your notes and compare them to the answers on the theme-analysis template above. Based upon my personal experience, I'm guessing that the answers on the template offer substantially more insight into the story's themes than do your notes from the read-though.

REVISON TO-DO LIST

Earlier in this chapter, I listed a series of troubleshooting techniques, which included a revision to-do list. Using my answers to the theme-analysis template as a guide, my revision to-do list for *Puss in Boots* includes the following.

- Establish more admirable goals for the protagonist than obtaining wealth and power.
- Instead of relying on lying and trickery as the primary means of achieving the story goal, establish more admirable means, and thus a more admirable theme.

With the other troubleshooting techniques in mind, I also add the following to the revision to-do list for this story.

- Develop a premise for the story.
- Write a one-paragraph summary of the story.
- To expand the scope of the story to novella length and more fully develop the plot to include additional plots, subplots, scenes, and sequels.
- Write a chapter-by-chapter outline of the story.
- Write a scene-and-sequel analysis.
- More fully develop the main characters of the story.
- More fully develop the setting of the story.
- Use fiction-writing-mode analysis to use more fully all eleven of the modes.
- Convert the style of the story from omniscient narration to intimate third-person narration, possibly with several viewpoint characters.

TAKEAWAYS

- A theme-analysis template is a structured means for systematically identifying and categorizing the themes of a story, a useful technique for troubleshooting a story.

The next chapter addresses fiction that matters.

17

FICTION THAT MATTERS

What are the essential elements for crafting fiction that truly matters? The answer, I believe, resides in the intricacies of a story's themes, especially in their profound impact on the reader. This impact can be most effectively viewed through the lenses of the heart, the mind, and the craft of storytelling to see what creates transcendence.

To qualify as transcendent, a novel must touch the heart: it must generate emotion, which may range from happiness to horror, intrigue to love, sadness to suspense. If the work of fiction isn't entertaining, the reader isn't likely to finish it, much less recall it in a positive way. To be transcendent, fiction must satisfy at least one audience, presumably the author's intended readers, whether that be the consumers of general fiction or a particular genre or subgenre. An example of transcendent fiction is Matt Haig's *The Midnight Library*, which takes the main character through an unforgettable roller coaster of emotions, which every fiction reader should experience.

If a novel is entertaining enough, it may not need much else. One of my favorite pastries is the plain-cake donut, which I find to be the perfect complement to a cup of coffee as I read or write. On the other hand, I really love carrot cake, which includes a variety of additional ingredients and is topped with delicious frosting. Likewise, an entertaining novel can be made even better if it also stimulates the mind. Regarding the intellectual effect of affirmation, Donald Maass notes that "Readers want to have their values validated ... but usually not in simplistic, moralizing ways. They may not want to be converted, but they do want to be stretched. They want to feel that at the end of the book their views were right but that they were arrived at after a struggle. A skillful breakout novelist can even spin a tale so persuasive that at the end, the reader feels the underlying point was one with which they always have agreed, even though they may never before considered it."[1] An example of such a novel is Jodi Picoult's *Wish You Were Here*, which "affirms" reader suspicions that time may indeed be multi-dimensional.

In addition to causing readers to be entertained and to having their beliefs validated, transcendent novels may affect readers in any number of other ways, such as to (1) acquire new information through education, (2) learn new skills through instruction, and (3) make sense of the world through elucidation. My favorite novels include historical fiction that portrays past events accurately, includes the demonstration of skills used in the past, and provides insight as to what life was like at that time. Examples include novels written by Bernard Cornwell (Napoleonic warfare and the Vikings) and Dewey Lambdin (sailing-ship warfare). If you are a fan of historical fiction, please consider *Backlash: A War of 1812 Novel* by yours truly.

Some transcendent novels reach an even higher plane by lifting and broadening the human spirit through inspiration or by inciting readers to action through motivation. A current example is Colleen Hoover's *It Ends With Us*, which I suspect provides inspiration for victims of domestic abuse and, I hope, motivation to address the issue.

Emotion, affirmation, education, instruction, elucidation, inspiration, and motivation are still not enough. To achieve transcendence, a writer must skillfully craft fiction to exceed reader expectations for each of the novel's fundamental themes of plot, character, setting, theme, and style. In other words, by making the story fascinating.

Donald Maass asks readers to think about their favorite novels and what they liked about them, and he then writes that the character experiences unusual, dramatic, and meaningful events throughout the story. A compelling narrative is marked by impactful occurrences, not necessarily wars or marvels, but events that significantly affect the characters. The actions or inactions of the characters play a crucial role in the novel, reflecting a universal struggle for reconciliation.[2] A great example of such a novel is Sara Gruin's *Water for Elephants*, which is filled with unusual, dramatic, and meaningful events.

Also, about your favorite novels, Maass refers to unforgettable characters, especially the great ones, that possess a larger-than-life quality. They behave, speak, and think in manners beyond our usual capabilities. These characters articulate what we aspire to say, engage in actions we dream about, and undergo the growth and transformation we wish for ourselves. They authentically experience emotions without avoidance, expressing our profound purposes and deepest desires. Ultimately, these characters resonate with us because they embody aspects of who we are.[3] An example of such a novel is Taylor Jenkins Reid's *The Seven Husbands of Evelyn Hugo*.

Regarding the setting of breakout novels, Maass also notes that they captivate you, carrying you off into their realms, transporting you to different eras or locations, and keeping you engrossed. Being transported elsewhere is a hallmark of exceptional fiction, involving the creation of a convincing, immersive, and compelling fictional world that stands distinct and complete on its own. This experience is unique, diverging from the ordinary and offering a perspective that many may not have or, if they do, one that they haven't intimately encountered.[4] An example of such a novel is *Outlander* by Diana Gabaldon.

Regarding theme, Maass refers to novels that have had a profound impact on your life, altering your perspective on the world. Even if they didn't necessarily change your opinions or beliefs, they likely revealed aspects of humanity, or perhaps divinity, that you hadn't previously recognized. These novels convey a message, offering a unique outlook, and are written with the author's passionate desire to make you understand, introduce you to someone special, or take you to a place of significance. Breakout novels are not neutral; they stir, challenge, confront, and illuminate. They are detailed because they reflect reality, with characters that live and breathe because they are drawn from life. These stories engage with our hopes, delve into our fears, test our faiths, and embody our human wills. What sets these novels apart is the authors' willingness to delve into their deepest selves without reservation, holding nothing back and making their works the most profound expression of their own experiences and beliefs. The prose in these novels serves a purpose.[5] An example of such a novel is Mitch Albom's *The Stranger in the Lifeboat*.

Permeating everything in a novel, style includes the multitude of choices fiction writers make, consciously or not. They encompass big picture, strategic issues such as point of view and narrator, but they also include the nitty-gritty, tactical choices of grammar, punctuation, word usage, sentence and paragraph length and structure, tone, the use of imagery, chapter selection, titles, and on and on. In the process of creating a story, these choices meld to become the writer's voice, his or her own unique style. In some novels, style stands out, for example, Colson Whitehead's Pulitzer Prize-winning *The Underground Railroad*. In others, style is so unobtrusive that the other aspects of fiction shine through with extra clarity, magnifying their effect. Many of the novels used as examples in this book are narrated in the first person. My book *Third-Person Possessed* addresses unobtrusive, intimate third-person narration.

In order to reach transcendence, a novel needs one more quality, and that is originality. Does originality mean something must be genuinely new? asks Donald Maass. Not necessarily.[6] "Although human nature may never change, our ways of looking at it will. To break out with familiar subject matter—and, really, it has all been written about before—it is essential to find a fresh angle. There certainly are no new plots. Not a one. There are also no settings that have not been used, and no professions that have not been given to protagonists. This is disheartening, but it is also a challenge. Working out an original approach can be highly rewarding."[7] Each of the bestselling novels presented as examples in this book displayed remarkable creativity.

TAKEAWAYS

- The answer to the question of how to write a novel that matters lies within a story's themes, particularly their effect on the reader, which may be best explained from the perspective of the heart, the mind, and the craft.
- To qualify as transcendent, a novel must touch the heart. It must generate emotion.
- Fiction may challenge a reader's beliefs, but in the end the readers want their beliefs to be validated.
- Transcendent novels may affect readers in other ways, such as to (1) acquire new information through education, (2) learn new skills through instruction, and (3) make sense of the world around us through elucidation.
- Some transcendent novels reach an even higher plane by lifting and broadening the human spirit through

inspiration or by inciting readers to action through motivation.
- Regarding the fundamental theme of plot, what happens to the character must be unusual, dramatic, and meaningful.
- The characters in a story must be those whom the reader cannot forget.
- Transcendent fiction transports the reader into a world that is different from what the reader usually experiences.
- Transcendent fiction alters the way a reader perceives the world.
- Some transcendent fiction features a style that stands on its own, while in others style is so unobtrusive that the other aspects of fiction shine through with extra clarity.
- Creating something really new may be difficult to achieve in written fiction, but originality may be achieved by developing a fresh approach to the subject matter.

I believe that understanding how to write fiction that matters is best achieved through the perspective of a story's theme. At the beginning, I stated that this book explores theme as never before, not only studying what theme is, but how it functions, how it can be analyzed, and how it can be developed so the story matters. Whether you are a writer, a teacher, or a student of the craft of writing fiction, I hope this information helps you achieve your objectives.

As a parting thought, I offer the following. Every story we tell, every novel we write, is a step towards understanding ourselves and the world around us. It's like building a bridge between hearts and minds.

Best wishes.

SHARE YOUR JOURNEY

Congratulations! You're now equipped with the insights to craft stories that resonate deeply and linger in the heart and mind of readers. As a writer, teacher, or student of fiction, you've gained valuable tools to shape tales that truly matter.

But your journey doesn't end here. It's time to extend a guiding hand to others on their path to storytelling excellence. By sharing your thoughts about *How to Write a Novel That Matters* on Amazon, you offer a beacon to fellow writers searching for direction. Your review is more than just words; it's a signpost for those seeking to enrich their craft, to weave tales that captivate, enlighten, and inspire.

To share your thoughts and help a fellow writer, just follow these easy steps. It's quick. Just scan the QR code below to leave your review:

https://www.amazon.com/review/create-review/?asin=B0CV82FJT3

If you feel the joy of assisting another writer, then welcome to our community of storytellers. You're now part of something bigger.

Thank you!
—Mike Klaassen

P.S. Remember, sharing knowledge is a gift that enriches both the giver and the receiver. If you think this book can assist another writer, teacher, or student of fiction, pass it along. Let's spread the wisdom and joy of storytelling.

ALSO BY MIKE KLAASSEN

NONFICTION

Third-Person Possessed: How to Write Page-Turning Fiction for 21st Century Readers

Scenes and Sequels: How to Write Page-Turning Fiction

Fiction-Writing Modes: Eleven Essential Tools for Bringing Your Story to Life

HISTORICAL FICTION

Backlash: A War of 1812 Novel

YOUNG-ADULT NOVELS

Cracks

The Brute

KLAASSEN'S CLASSIC FOLKTALES

Jack and the Beanstalk: The Old English Story Told as a Novella

Cinderella: The Brothers Grimm Story Told as a Novella

The Frog Prince: The Brothers Grimm Story Told as a Novella

Hansel and Gretel: The Brothers Grimm Story Told as a Novella

ABOUT THE AUTHOR

Mike Klaassen crafts thought-provoking, action-packed stories about young protagonists grappling with formidable challenges. His three novels, *The Brute*, *Cracks*, and *Backlash: A War of 1812 Novel*, each earned a B.R.A.G. Medallion, distinguishing them for their quality among independent publications.

Driven by a passion for continuous learning and research, Mike delved into the art of storytelling, producing a series of insightful books about the craft of writing fiction. These works not only offer practical guidance for aspiring writers but also illuminate the intricate processes behind compelling storytelling.

Fusing his love for folklore and his expertise in fiction, Mike initiated "Klaassen's Classic Folktales," which retells ancient stories as engaging novellas. Through this collection, he breathes new life into time-honored tales, offering readers, both young and old, a fresh perspective on these enduring stories.

BIBLIOGRAPHY

Aristotle. *Poetics*. Translated with an introduction and notes by Malcolm Heath. New York: Penguin Books, 1996. ISBN: 9780140446364.

Bell, James Scott. *Revision & Self Editing: Techniques for Transforming Your First Draft into a Finished Novel*. Cincinnati: Writer's Digest Books, 2008. ISBN: 9781582975092.

Bishop, Leonard. *Dare to Be a Great Writer*. Cincinnati: Writer's Digest Books, 1988. ISBN: 9780898793123.

Egri, Lajos. *The Art of Dramatic Writing: Its Basis in the Creative Interpretation of Human Motives*. New York: Simon & Schuster, 1942. ISBN: 9780671213329.

Faulkner, William. *As I Lay Dying: The Corrected Text*. Reissue edition. New York: Vintage, 1991. ISBN: 9780679732259.

Forster, E. M. *Aspects of the Novel*. New York: Harcourt, Inc., 1927. ISBN: 9780156091800.

Frey, James N. *How to Write a Damn Good Novel: A Step-by-Step No Nonsense Guide to Dramatic Storytelling*. New York: St. Martin's Press, 1987. ISBN: 9780312010447.

Freytag, Gustav. *Freytag's Technique of Drama: An Exposition of Dramatic Composition and Art*. Chicago: Forgotten Books, Classic reprint series, 1894. ASIN: B008HL7RMI.

Gardner, John. *The Art of Fiction: Notes on Craft for Young Writers*. New York: Vintage Books, 1984. ISBN: 9780679734031.

Gardner, John. *On Becoming a Novelist*. New York: W. W. Norton & Company, 1983. ISBN: 9780393320039.

Gardner, John. *On Moral Fiction*. New York: Basic Books, Perseus Books Group, 1978 and 2000. ISBN: 9780465052264.

Garmus, Bonnie. *Lessons in Chemistry*. New York: Doubleday, 2022. ISBN: 9780385547345.

Gotham Writers' Workshop. *Writing Fiction: The Practical Guide from New York's Acclaimed Creative Writing School*. New York: Bloomsbury, 2003. ISBN: 9781582343303.

www.grimmstories.com/en/grimm_fairy-tales/puss_in_boots. June 15, 2021.

Grisham, John. *A Time for Mercy*. New York: Doubleday, 2020. ISBN: 9780385545969.

Guthrie, A. B., Jr. *A Field Guide to Writing Fiction*. New York: Harper-Collins Publishers, 1991. ISBN: 9780062700025.

Hannah, Kristin. *The Four Winds*. New York: St. Martin's Press, 2021. ISBN: 9781250178602.

Harper, Steven. "Weaving Theme into Speculative Fiction." *Writer's Digest*, March/April 2014, 57-58.

Hoover, Colleen. *It Ends With Us*. New York: Atria Paperback, 2016. ISBN: 9781501110368.

James, Steven. *Story Trumps Structure: How to Write Unforgettable Fiction by Breaking the Rules*. Cincinnati: Writer's Digest Books, 2014. ISBN: 9781599636511.

www.jodipicoult.com, March 25, 2023.

Kempton, Gloria. *Dialogue: Techniques and Exercises for Crafting Effective Dialogue (Write Great Fiction Series)*. Cincinnati: Writer's Digest Books, 2004. ISBN: 9781582972893.

Klaassen, Mike. *Fiction-Writing Modes: Eleven Essential Tools for Bringing Your Story to Life*. Pennsauken, NJ: Bookbaby, 2015. ISBN: 9781682221006.

Klaassen, Mike. "The Fifth Element: The 'Other Stuff' of Fiction." Helium.com, August 23, 2007.

Klaassen, Mike. *Scenes and Sequels: How to Write Page-Turning Fiction*. Pennsauken, NJ: Bookbaby, 2016. ISBN: 9781682229071.

Klaassen, Mike. *Third-Person Possessed*. Pennsauken, NJ: Bookbaby, 2020. ISBN: 9781734488739.

Kress, Nancy. *Dynamic Characters*. Cincinnati: Writer's Digest Books, 1998. ISBN: 9781582973197.

Lukeman, Noah. *The Plot Thickens*. New York: St Martins Griffen, 2002. ISBN: 9780312309282.

Maass, Donald. *Writing the Breakout Novel*. Cincinnati: Writer's Digest Books, 2001. ISBN: 9780898799958.

Marshall, Evan. *The Marshall Plan for Novel Writing: A 16-Step Program Guaranteed to Take You from Idea to Completed Manuscript*. Paperback edition. Cincinnati: Writer's Digest Books, 1998. ISBN: 9781582970622.

McKee, Robert. *Story: Substance, Structure, Style, and the Principles of Screenwriting*. New York: ReganBooks, 1997. ISBN: 9780060391683.

www.merriam-webster.com/dictionary.

Morrell, Jessica Page. *Between the Lines: Master the Subtle Elements of Fiction Writing*. Cincinnati: Writer's Digest Books, 2006. ISBN: 9781582973937.

Obstfeld, Raymond. *Fiction First Aid*. Cincinnati: Writer's Digest Books, 2002. ISBN: 9781582971179.

O'hara, John. Safire, William and Leonard Safir. *Good Advice on Writing: Great Quotations from Writers Past and Present on How to Write Well*. New York: Simon & Schuster, 1992, 251. ISBN: 9780671872335.

Owens, Delia. *Where the Crawdads Sing*. New York: Random House, 2018. ISBN: 9781984827616.

Picoult, Jodi. *Wish You Were Here*. New York: Balantine Books, 2021. ISBN: 9781984818416.

Poe, Edgar Allan. "The Importance of the Single Effect in a Prose Tale." Philadelphia: *Graham's Magazine*, May 1842. http://msnovickenglish.weebly.com/uploads/1/3/5/5/13557192/single_effect_poe.pdf

Poe, Edgar Allan. "The Philosophy of Composition." www.poetryfoundation.org/articles/69390/the-philosophy-of-composition

www.poetryfoundation.org/poems/46957/little-miss-muffet.

Reid, Mildred. "Only One 'Must,'" February 1950. *The Writer's Digest Guide to Good Writing*. Cincinnati: Writer's Digest Books, 1994. ISBN: 9780898796407.

Reissenweber, Brandi. "Ask the Writer: Does a story have to have a moral?" *The Writer*, May 2011, 8.

Safire, William and Leonard Safir. *Good Advice on Writing: Great Quotations from Writers Past and Present on How to Write Well*. New York: Simon & Schuster, 1992, 251. ISBN: 9780671872335.

Schmidt, Victoria Lynn. *45 Master Characters: Mythic Models for Creating Original Characters*. Cincinnati: Writer's Digest Books, 2001. ISBN: 9781582970691.

Selgin, Peter. *By Cunning & Craft: Sound Advice and Practical Wisdom for Fiction Writers*. Cincinnati: Writer's Digest Books, 2007. ISBN: 9781582974910.

Serle, Rebecca. *One Italian Summer*. New York: Atria Books, 2022. ISBN: 9781982166793.

Swain, Dwight V. *Techniques of the Selling Writer*. Norman: University of Oklahoma Press, 1965. ISBN: 9780806111919.

Tobias, Ronald B. *Theme and Strategy*. Cincinnati: Writer's Digest Books, 1989. ISBN: 9780898793925.

Tobias, Ronald B. *20 Master Plots (And How to Build Them)*. Cincinnati: Writer's Digest Books, 1993. ISBN: 9780898795950.

Thom, James Alexander. *The Art and Craft of Writing Historical Fiction*. Cincinnati: Writer's Digest Books, 2010. ISBN: 9781582975696.

Truby, John. *The Anatomy of Story: 22 Steps to Becoming a Master Storyteller*. New York: Faber and Faber, Inc., 2007. ISBN: 9780865479517.

Vorhaus, John. *The Comic Toolbox*. Los Angeles: Silman-James Press, 1994. ISBN: 9781879505216.

Webster's Third New International Dictionary of the English Language, Unabridged. Springfield, MA: Merriam-Webster, Inc., 2002. ISBN: 9780877790013.

Writer's Digest Guide to Good Writing. Cincinnati: Writer's Digest Books, 1994. ISBN: 9780898796407.

INDEX

act, 13
adage, 93
affirmation, 19
affirmative, 20
allegoric message, 92
allegory, 54
analysis, 26
aphorism, 93
archetype, 31
Aristotelian themes, 91
art, 15
bromide, 93
call to action, 26
case study, 54
cause-and-effect statement, 92
chapter, 13
chapter-by-chapter outline, 140
character, 13, 30
character arc, 31
characteristic, 30
characterization, 30, 54
chronicle of events, 54
chronicle, 25
chronological timeline, 37
climax, 27
combined theme statement, 95
comedy, 56
complex story, 60
complex, compound story, 60
compound story, 60
condensation, 19

craft, 15
creativity, 38
crisis, 27
crucible, 26, 33
dark moment, 27
definition of theme, 11
demonstration, 54
denouement, 27
dilemma, 26
education, 21
educational, 21
effectiveness, 37, 71
elucidation, 22
elucidative, 22
emotion, 18, 26
emotive, 18
explicitness, 68
external plot, 28
fiction-writing mode, 44
fiction-writing-mode analysis, 140
fundamental elements, 7, 13
genre, 39
if you...then you... message, 92
if-then, 92
ignore theme, 8
imperative sentence, 92
implicitness, 71
inciting incident, 26
inciting-incident, 89
inspiration, 22
inspirational, 22
instruction, 21
instructive, 21
intentionality, 66
internal plot, 28
ironic, 57

linear, 33
macro-themes, 12
main plot, 60
man-versus-nature, 33
man-versus-society, 33
master plot, 28
maxim, 93
meso-themes, 12
message, 43
message theme, 43
micro-themes, 12
milieu, 32
motif, 51
motivation, 23
motivational, 23
nocuousness, 67
obtrusiveness, 68
one-paragraph summary, 140
opinion dump, 68
opposition, 89
optimistic, 57
orientation, 26
originality, 71
parallel, 33
parallel plots, 60
passage of writing, 12, 95
personal message, 92
pessimistic, 57
platitude, 93
plot, 13, 25
premise, 90, 140
profundity, 50, 72
propaganda, 64
prototype plot, 26
proverb, 93
read-through, 140

208 | INDEX

refutative, 20
repetition, 51
resolution, 27
resonance, 72
resonate, 7
revision to-do list, 140
rising action, 27
saw, 93
scene-and-sequel analysis, 140
segment of writing, 12
selection, 19
setting, 13, 32
setup, 26
simple story, 59
situational symbol, 48
skill, 38
slice of life, 54
story, 55
story message, 56
structural themes, 11
structural units of fiction, 13
style, 13, 36
subplot, 60
suspend disbelief, 37
symbol, 47
theme, 13
theme-analysis template, 105, 140
themes of effect, 12
thinking, 26
ticking clock, 33
time, 33
tragedy, 56
transcendence, 7
transcendent, 150
travelogue, 54
troubleshoot, 133
truthfulness, 67

universal symbol, 47
validation, 19
visualization, 27
what if..., 89
worldview, 66
zeitgeist, 32

NOTES

INSPIRATION

1. Kress, 247.

1. INTRODUCTION

1. Lukeman, 186.
2. Gardner, *The Art of Fiction*, 13.
3. Klaassen, "The Fifth Element," Helium.com, August 23, 2007.
4. Marshall, 142.
5. *Webster's*, resonance.

2. DEFINING THEME

1. Klaassen, *Fiction-Writing Modes*, 180.
2. Klaassen, *Scenes and Sequels*, 77.
3. Klaassen, *Third-Person Possessed*, 24.
4. Klaassen, *Fiction-Writing Modes*, 180.
5. Klaassen, "The Fifth Element," Helium.com, August 23, 2007.
6. Klaassen, "The Fifth Element," Helium.com, August 23, 2007.

3. FICTION AS ART

1. Aristotle, 4.
2. Poe, "The Philosophy of Composition," 4-5.
3. Gardner, *On Moral Fiction*, 128.
4. Egri, xv.
5. Egri, xiv.
6. Egri, xv.
7. Reid, *Writer's Digest Guide to Good Writing*, 105.

8. Gardner, *On Moral Fiction*, 112.
9. Hannah, 425.
10. Gardener, *On Moral Fiction*, 112.
11. Gotham, 14.
12. Swain, 129-130.
13. Gardner, *On Moral Fiction*, 131.
14. Gardner, *On Moral Fiction*, 146.
15. Kempton, 223.
16. Maass, 237.
17. *Webster's*, refutative.
18. Kempton, 222.
19. Gardner, *On Moral Fiction*, 39.
20. Gardner, *On Moral Fiction*, 39.
21. Gardner, *On Moral Fiction*, 42.
22. Lukeman, 200.
23. Thom, 237.
24. Gardner, *On Moral Fiction*, 27.
25. Lukeman, 200.
26. Lukeman, 200.
27. Kempton, 219.
28. Kempton, 225.
29. Poe, "The Philosophy of Composition," 5.

4. THEMES OF PLOT, CHARACTER, SETTING, AND STYLE

1. Klaassen, *Fiction-Writing Modes*, 4.
2. Klaassen, *Third-Person Possessed*, 16.
3. James, 15-16.
4. Freytag, 108.
5. McKee, 181, 189-194.
6. Freytag, 66.
7. Swain, 201.
8. Freytag, 35.
9. Freytag, 34.
10. Forster, 37.
11. Freytag, 20.
12. Freytag, 9, 20, and 252.

13. Klaassen, *Fiction-Writing Modes*, 4.
14. Freytag, 20.
15. Freytag, 9, 20, and 252.
16. Klaassen, *Fiction-Writing Modes*, 4.
17. Safire, 251.
18. Tobias, *Theme and Strategy*, 100-101.
19. *Webster's*, characterization.
20. *Webster's*, characteristic.
21. *Webster's*, archetype.
22. Webster's, archetype.
23. Schmidt, 9.
24. Klaassen, *Fiction-Writing Modes*, 4.
25. *Webster's*, characterization.
26. *Webster's*, characteristic.
27. *Webster's*, archetype.
28. Webster's, archetype.
29. Klaassen, *Fiction-Writing Modes*, 4.
30. *Webster's*, zeitgeist.
31. Klaassen, *Fiction-Writing Modes*, 4.
32. *Webster's*, zeitgeist
33. Gardner, *The Art of Fiction*, 75.
34. Klaassen, *Fiction-Writing Modes*, 4.
35. Tobias, *Theme and Strategy*, 100.
36. Klaassen, *Fiction-Writing Modes*, 4.
37. Faulkner, 8.
38. Klaassen, *Fiction-Writing Modes*, 4.
39. Klaassen, *Fiction-Writing Modes*, 4.

5. GENRE

1. Gardner, *The Art of Fiction*, 18.
2. *Webster's*, genre.
3. *Webster's*, fable.
4. *Webster's*, parable.
5. *Webster's*, satire.
6. *Webster's*, genre.

6. MESSAGE THEMES, PART 1—FICTION-WRITING MODES

1. Klaassen, *Fiction-Writing Modes*, 4.
2. Gardner, *On Moral Fiction*, 60.
3. Gardner, *On Moral Fiction*, 193.
4. Hannah, 3.
5. Klaassen, *Fiction-Writing Modes*, 3.
6. Garmus, 109.
7. Serle, 191.
8. Hoover, 321.

7. MESSAGE THEMES, PART 2—SYMBOLS

1. Bishop, 311.
2. Maass, 235.
3. Lukeman, 195-196.
4. Obstfeld, 178.
5. Bishop, 309-310.
6. Obstfeld, 178.
7. Obstfeld, 178.
8. Obstfeld, 178.
9. Obstfeld, 178.
10. Obstfeld, 179.
11. Obstfeld, 179.
12. Obstfeld, 178.
13. Obstfeld, 178.
14. Obstfeld, 178.
15. Obstfeld, 177.
16. Bishop, 309-310.
17. Obstfeld, 177.
18. Bishop, 311.
19. Obstfeld, 177.
20. Obstfeld, 177.
21. Bishop, 311.
22. Lukeman, 197.
23. Gardner, *On Moral Fiction*, 121.

24. Maass, 235.
25. Bishop, 311.
26. Maass, 235-236.
27. Bishop, 311.
28. Bishop, 311.
29. Obstfeld, 178.
30. Obstfeld, 178.
31. Obstfeld, 178.
32. Gardner, *On Moral Fiction*, 121.
33. Bishop, 311.
34. Bishop, 311.

8. MESSAGE THEMES, PART 3—ALLEGORY

1. *Webster's*, allegory.
2. Klaassen, *Third-Person Possessed*, 12.
3. Klaassen, *Third-Person Possessed*, 13.
4. Klaassen, *Third-Person Possessed*, 13.
5. Klaassen, *Third-Person Possessed*, 13-14.
6. Aristotle, 8-9.
7. McKee, 122.
8. McKee, 123.
9. McKee, 124.
10. McKee, 125.
11. McKee, 128.
12. McKee, 125-126.
13. McKee, 126-127.
14. *Webster's*, allegory.

9. MESSAGE VS. PROPAGANDA

1. Gardner, *On Moral Fiction*, 60.
2. www.merriam-webster.com/dictionary/propaganda, "The History of Propaganda," January 20, 2023.
3. *Webster's*, propaganda.
4. Gardner, *On Moral Fiction*, 107.
5. Gardner, *On Moral Fiction*, 106.

6. Gardner, *On Moral Fiction*, 106.
7. Kress, 248.
8. *Webster's,* nocuous.
9. *Webster's,* innocuous.
10. *Webster's,* explicit.
11. Garmus, 14.
12. Garmus, 26.
13. Garmus, 39.
14. *Webster's,* implicit.
15. Hannah, 447.
16. Hannah, 448.
17. Maass, 242.
18. Maass, 242.
19. Gardner, *On Moral Fiction*, 173.
20. Lukeman, 197.
21. *Webster's, profound.*
22. Maass, 241.
23. Hoover, 372.
24. www.merriam-webster.com/dictionary/propaganda, "The History of Propaganda," January 20, 2023.
25. *Webster's, propaganda.*

10. STRATEGIES FOR MESSAGE DEVELOPMENT

1. Reissenweber, 8.
2. Reissenweber, 8.
3. Guthrie, 77.
4. Poe, "The Philosophy of Composition," 3.
5. Selgin, 182.
6. Poe, "The Philosophy of Composition," 3.
7. Tobias, *Theme and Strategy*, 97.
8. Poe, "Edgar Allan: The Importance of the Single Effect in a Prose Tale," 1.
9. Selgin, 187.
10. Gardner, *On Moral Fiction*, 124.
11. McKee, 113.
12. Obstfeld, 176.
13. Bell, 178.

14. Tobias, *Theme and Strategy*, 110-111.
15. Obstfeld, 176.
16. McKee, 115-117 and 130-131.
17. McKee, 115-117 and 130-131.
18. Harper, 57-58.
19. Bell, 179.
20. Frey, 61.
21. Obstfeld, 176.
22. Bell, 180.
23. Bell, 180.
24. Kress, 252.
25. Selgin, 182.

11. EXPRESSING THEME

1. Morrell, 278.
2. Tobias, 183.
3. Schmidt, 9.
4. *Webster's*, premise.
5. Truby, 16.
6. Truby, 17.
7. Vorhaus, 99.
8. Vorhaus, 147.
9. *Webster's*, aphorism.
10. www.thoughtco.com/what-is-a-maxim-p2-1691778, April 20, 2023.
11. *Webster's*, platitude.

12. ANALYSIS OF A BESTSELLER

1. www.jodipicoult.com, March 25, 2023.
2. Picoult, 4-11.
3. Picoult, 20.
4. Picoult, 187.
5. Picoult, 3.
6. Picoult, 270.
7. www.jodipicoult.com, March 25, 2023.

14. THEME-ANALYSIS TEMPLATE—SIMPLE STORY

1. www.poetryfoundation.org/poems/46957/little-miss-muffet. April 20, 2023.

15. THEME-ANALYSIS TEMPLATE—COMPLEX STORY

1. Owens, 111.

16. TROUBLESHOOTING A MANUSCRIPT FOR THEME

1. www.grimmstories.com/*en/grimm_fairy-tales/puss_in_boots*. June 15, 2021.

17. FICTION THAT MATTERS

1. Maass, 230.
2. Maass, 37.
3. Maass, 37-38.
4. Maass, 37.
5. Maass, 39.
6. Maass, 42.
7. Maass, 43.

Made in the USA
Las Vegas, NV
22 July 2025